10 Minute Guide to Job Interviews

by Dana Morgan

A Division of Macmillan Publishing
A Simon & Schuster Macmillan Company
1633 Broadway, New York, NY 10019-6785

Editor: Eve Steinberg
Production Editor: Michael Thomas
Copy Editor: Erik Dafforn
Cover Designer: Dan Armstrong
Designer: Glenn Larsen
Indexer: Nadia Ibrahim
Production Team: Tricia Flodder, Angela Perry, Megan Wade

This Indian Edition 1999

This low priced edition is published by arrangement with ***Macmillan, New York, USA,*** **for sale in India only.** This is the only authorised, complete and unabridged reprint of the latest American edition.

Published by Ashwani Goyal for
W.R. GOYAL Publishers & Distributors
86 U.B. Jawahar Nagar, Delhi-110007 (India)
E-Mail : goylsaab@del2.vsnl.net.in

Distributed by ***General Book Depot***
1691, Nai Sarak, Delhi - 110006.
Tel : 3263695, 3250635 Fax : 011-2940861

Printed by Gopsons Paper Ltd., Noida.

Contents

Introduction vi

1 **Getting Started** 1

The Interviewing Process Today 2
Preparation Is Key 3
The Six Areas of Readiness 4
Summary 5

2 **Evaluating Your Skills** 6

Identify Your Major Accomplishments 7
Accomplishments Involve Skills 7
The Two Types of Skills 8
The Four-Step Skills Assessment Exercise 10
Summary 13

3 **The Two-Minute Bio** 14

Guidelines to a Good Bio 15
Sample Two-Minute Bios 15
Creating Your Own Two-Minute Bio 17
Summary 18

4 **Preparing for the Interview** 19

Pre-Interview Preparation Techniques: Empower Yourself! 19
What to Bring to the Interview 25
Summary 25

5 **Types of Interviews** 26

The Three Levels of Interviews 27
Summary 30

6 **Alternative Interview Formats** 31

The Telephone Interview 31
The Stress Interview 33
The Panel Interview 35
The Interview with a Meal 37
Summary 38

7 **What Hiring Managers Look For** 39

Evaluating Job Candidates 40
The Eight Personal Qualities Hiring Managers Look for Most 41
Company Baggage 45
Summary 47

8 Dress Guidelines for Visual Impact 48

How to Look Your Best for an Interview 48
Tips For a Polished Look 49
Dress Guidelines for Men 50
Dress Guidelines for Women 52
Summary 54

9 Projecting Success 55

The Professional Image 55
Personal Preparation Before the Interview 55
Projecting Success: The Beginning of the Interview 56
Projecting Success: The Middle of the Interview 59
Projecting Success: The End of the Interview 60
Summary 61

10 Interviewing Strategies 62

14 Rules of Thumb for the Job Interview 62
14 Things to Avoid in the Interview 66
Summary 68

11 Interviewing Hazards and How to Overcome Them 69

10 Common Interviewing Hazards 69
Summary 77

12 Questions to Answer 78

The Interviewer's Task 78
The Eight Keys to Answering Interview Questions 79
Some Basic Questions You'll Probably Hear 81
The Tough Questions 86
Summary 89

13 Using Examples 90

Prove It 90
Prove the Right Thing 91
Exercise 1: Answering Questions with Examples of Experience 92
Exercise 2: Matching Your Experiences to Skills 94
Summary 95

14 Questions to Ask 96

Tips for Asking Questions 96
Questions that Sell 98
Questions that Buy 100
The Three Key Aspects of the Job 101
Summary 102

15 **ILLEGAL QUESTIONS** 103
Legal Guidelines 103
How to Respond to Illegal Questions 107
Summary 108

16 **THE THANK-YOU NOTE** 109
When to Write a Thank-You Note 109
Who Should be Sent a Thank-You Letter? 110
The Proper Style for a Thank-You Letter 111
What to Include in Your Thank-You Letter 112
Following Up 116
Examples 117
Summary 118

17 **SALARY NEGOTIATION** 119
The Seven Rules to Remember When Negotiating Salary 120
How to Play the Range Game at Offer Time 126
Summary 127

18 **BENEFITS PACKAGES** 128
Negotiating Beyond Salary 128
Benefits Your Package May Include 130
Summary 132

19 **EVALUATING THE JOB OFFER** 133
The Eight Most Important Aspects to Consider in a Job Offer 134
Don't Set Your Sights Too Low 136
Generating Multiple Offers 136
Weighing Multiple Offers 138
Accepting a New Position 138
Resigning from Your Current Position 139
Summary 139

A **FINDING INFORMATION ON COMPANIES: PRINTED SOURCES OF CORPORATE PROFILES** 140

B **FINDING INFORMATION ON COMPANIES: ONLINE SOURCES OF CORPORATE PROFILES** 145

C **LIST OF ADDITIONAL INTUITIVE AND LEARNED SKILLS** 147

INDEX 150

INTRODUCTION

The job interview is a ritual that requires practice and polish whether you are a novice or a veteran to the process. *The 10 Minute Guide to Job Interviews* gives useful advice to any job seeker, no matter what the job level or the number of years in the workforce.

For the Novice *The 10 Minute Guide to Job Interviews* offers the key information you need to understand the interview process and to develop the basic skills and knowledge necessary for a successful interview performance.

For the Veteran *The 10 Minute Guide to Job Interviews* offers a refresher on interviewing tips and an update on the trends and expectations in the hiring arena today.

Whatever your background, *The 10 Minute Guide to Job Interviews* is designed to give you quick, easy, yet thorough guidelines to help you navigate the job interview process as smoothly and successfully as possible. As you read the lessons, you will learn the answers to these and other important questions:

- How can I present my background and skills in the best possible light?
- What are employers looking for when they interview job candidates?
- What should I do to prepare for an interview?
- What are some pitfalls I should avoid?
- How can I answer interview questions with confidence?
- How can I know whether an offer is good for me?

CONVENTIONS USED IN THIS BOOK

Throughout this book, three types of icons help you find important information quickly:

Timesaver Tip icons offer ideas that cut corners and avoid confusion.

Plain English icons define new terms.

Panic Button icons identify potential problem areas and how to solve them.

ACKNOWLEDGMENTS

To Joel, for providing helpful editing suggestions, a dependable listening ear, and fresh flowers every now and then.

To Kiera, Taylor, and Chase, for their patience and restraint. And to Gigi, for all her help.

To my parents, for their guidance and support.

To the professional and caring counselors and consultants at Manchester Partners, International.

To all the hard-working job seekers I have had the pleasure to work with. May you all achieve great success in your interviewing adventures!

ABOUT THE AUTHOR

Dana Morgan has worked on both sides of the desk in the interviewing process. She began her career as a placement counselor, helping graduating college students find their first jobs. She later worked as a recruiting specialist for the General Accounting Office in Washington, DC, helping to guide both entry- and senior-level job candidates through the interviewing process and bringing them on board with the federal government.

For the past six years she has owned her own business, *The Career Center,* in Columbia, MD, through which she consults and offers seminars and workshops on all topics related to the hiring process.

Her previous books include *Federal Jobs for College Graduates* (Arco Books, 1991) and *Federal Jobs, The Ultimate Guide* (Arco Books, 1996).

LESSON 1

GETTING STARTED

In this lesson you learn about the most recent trends in interviewing and get an overview of the most important aspects to prepare for in the interviewing process.

Imagine if job interviews didn't exist. No job seeker would have to suffer through a single agonizing interview moment. All hiring would simply be done by paperwork alone, through review of résumés or application forms. It would be less stressful, perhaps, but not very practical for anyone involved in the process.

The job interview may be challenging, tense, and sometimes downright unpleasant, but it does have its purpose: to introduce you, the job seeker, to the decision-maker, the person who wants to hire. It's a two-way street, meant to give the company a glance at you and to give you a glance at the company. Each of you, then, is formulating opinions and making decisions about the other.

The decision-maker is asking him- or herself:

- Do I want to hire the job candidate?
- Would the applicant fit in well with the other people in the office?
- Does the candidate have the skills we need to get the job done?

- Does the applicant have the right personality traits for the job (stamina, tenacity, assertiveness, and so on)?

You're asking yourself:

- Do I want to work for these people?
- Do I like the location, the size of the company, the atmosphere?
- Does the job sound like something I can handle?
- Can I grow here?

THE INTERVIEWING PROCESS TODAY

Interviewing for a job today is different in many ways from what it was just a few years ago. Here's how:

- *The process is longer.* Today's job seeker must typically endure three or more interviews before receiving an offer.
- *More people are involved.* Job interviews today are more likely to be conducted by a panel of people (two or more) rather than by just one individual.
- *The focus is on the person.* Today's job interviews focus more on personal motivations and qualities rather than on experience and job skills. Be prepared to answer tough, open-ended questions.
- *The interview can be an endurance test.* A new trend in job interviews is to test the candidate's mettle. Can he handle stress? Can she endure criticism?
- *There are more jobs at more levels.* The "company man" mentality is no longer the presiding mentality in the workplace. Turnover is common, even at the senior levels. A worker no longer assumes that his boss will be his boss until one of them retires.

Therefore, a wider selection of positions is available for a wider selection of candidates.

You've Got to Do Your Homework! As a consequence of the information explosion, potential employers expect job applicants to be more savvy, knowledgeable, and aware of industry trends than in past years.

- *There is more competition.* Because of high turnover, more applicants are applying for positions, yet the positions are less stable and often include a broader range of responsibilities than did positions in the past.

PREPARATION IS KEY

Companies expect today's applicants to be ready for the interview—ready for the tough questions and ready to ask a few tough questions of their own. Sitting passively in an interview does not make for success. There is a lot of work to be done, and when an interview is on the horizon, you have two choices:

- You can agonize and get stressed.
- Or, you can organize and get prepared.

Start Early Don't wait until you land an interview to begin preparing for it. Instead, start your interview preparations as soon as you begin your job search. Give yourself the time you need to do a thorough job.

The Six Areas of Readiness

A wise job seeker should cover six critical areas of preparation before any job interview. Getting familiar with these six areas helps to ensure success and lessen stress.

1. Know Yourself

We all feel perfectly confident that we know ourselves quite well—until it comes time to present ourselves in the concise and targeted format of a job interview. The ability to do this takes examination of our background, skills, accomplishments, and goals. It also takes a lot of practice and an occasional re-evaluation.

2. Know What You Need

Part of your self-examination should focus not on what you have to offer the company, but on what you want the company to offer you. Before an interview, you need to know your interests, your values, your career goals, and your salary requirements. Deciding these things during the interview or after the interview is too late.

3. Know How to Look the Part

The image you present when you walk through the interviewer's door, for better or worse, plays a large part in the hiring manager's decision-making process. Like it or not, you must work on your self-presentation so that only the best shines through.

4. Know the Company

This, at least, is an easier task than it used to be, now that so much information is available via computer. If you go into an interview without having learned about the company with which you're talking, you're likely to leave the interview with a red face and no offer.

5. Know the Interviewing Game

Winning sports teams take care to explore their opponent's strategies before each game. The interview process can be explored in the same way. What does the interviewer want to get from you in the interview? What tactics will be used to get it?

6. Know How to Answer and Ask the Right Questions

Few job interviews have taken place that have not involved a question-and-answer period, with both interviewer and interviewee actively engaged. Yet many job seekers unwisely approach the interview without having prepared answers to some of the most common interview questions. The results? A lot of stumbling, stammering, faltering, and certainly, regret.

As you read the lessons that follow, you will become thoroughly prepared in all six of the interview readiness areas.

Summary

In this lesson you learned the newest trends in job interviewing and the six key areas of interview preparation.

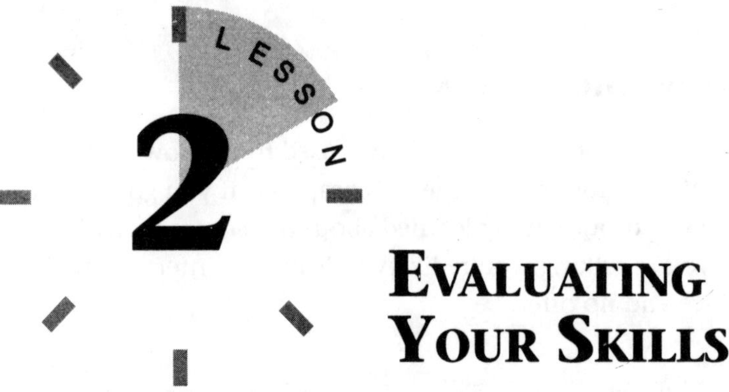

Evaluating Your Skills

In this lesson you learn to identify your most significant accomplishments and to determine what skills you used in achieving those accomplishments. This process is useful throughout all aspects of your job search and in the job interview itself.

A skillful job hunter knows who he is and what he has to offer. Remember that an interview is a sales situation, and the product you are selling is *you.* It would be unwise to meet your potential buyer without having first developed a thorough knowledge of your product.

In almost any interview, you can expect to be asked, "Why should we hire you?" or "What makes you stand out from our other applicants?" This is one of the most important questions you will be asked. It is the interviewer's way of trying to discern the special aspects of your background and personality that will enable you to be a high achiever on the job.

In order to answer this question well, you must do some preparation long before the interview begins. First you must study your accomplishments—the successes you have achieved throughout your life.

IDENTIFY YOUR MAJOR ACCOMPLISHMENTS

An accomplishment is something that:

- You did well
- You enjoyed doing
- Involved a problem that you solved
- You are proud of

Accomplishments begin with situations or problems that call for action. You have taken steps to alleviate the problems, thereby achieving results.

An accomplishment does not have to relate to your school or work experience. It can be anything from your personal background as well. Some examples are:

- Planned a trip and traveled to Europe solo
- Coordinated a conference for 180 people
- Directed the annual PTA fund-raiser

These are specific projects you took on either at work, school, home, or in the community.

Remember the Results Don't overlook the results portion of your accomplishments. Employers key in on results.

ACCOMPLISHMENTS INVOLVE SKILLS

You can't write a good poem without having good writing skills. You can't direct a successful program without having good leadership skills. Each of your accomplishments can be broken down into a set of skills that you used in realizing the accomplishment.

Don't Be Shy Employers want to know if you have the skills to accomplish a particular job for them. When you integrate some of your key accomplishments into the interview, employers will discern the skills that you have and assess whether you can put those same skills to use for them.

THE TWO TYPES OF SKILLS

Employers attempt to assess two types of skills during an interview:

1. LEARNED SKILLS

Learned Skills Skills that you have been taught or that you have taught yourself somewhere along the way in your life. They might be related to your current career, past positions, or other aspects of your life.

Examples of learned skills:

Rebuilding a car engine

Driving a bus

Planting a garden

Running a computer program

Hanging drywall

Sewing a dress

Managing a product line

All of these skills involve learning new behaviors and gaining knowledge about the way things work and the steps involved in making certain things happen. In none of these cases could a person know how to do these things without first learning how.

Stay Close to the Topic Learned skills are not necessarily technological or career-related. Cooking a gourmet dinner is just as much a learned skill as launching a satellite; both involve learned processes and behaviors. A potential employer, however, is most interested in the learned skills that are closely related to the position for which you are applying.

2. Intuitive Skills

Intuitive Skills Skills that you possess innately; they are a part of your personality, and you are able to use these skills in many different situations.

Examples of intuitive skills:

- Persistence
- Tidiness
- Efficiency
- Creativity
- Tenacity
- Honesty
- Precision
- Adaptability
- Punctuality

These are personality traits that you carry with you throughout life. As you can see, they are less specific than the learned skills, but they are no less important. These skills are transferable from one situation to the next: If you are honest in one situation you are likely to be honest in another. Punctual people can be counted on to arrive on time, no matter what the setting or situation.

Know Your Intuitive Skills Potential employers often pay more attention in the interview to intuitive skills than they do to learned skills. You must be ready with a defined skills list if you are to do well in the interview!

THE FOUR-STEP SKILLS ASSESSMENT EXERCISE

Identifying your own skills and strengths is not difficult. Follow through the four steps of this simple exercise and compile your personal skills list.

1. LIST YOUR SIX FAVORITE ACCOMPLISHMENTS.

These can be from any time period in your life and can be as detailed or simple as you wish. You might include accomplishments from a childhood scouting project, the time you stood up to the bully on the playground, or the million-dollar account you landed last July.

Example:

When I was 22 and had just graduated from college, I talked a group of my friends into spending 6 months with me on a backpacking trip of Europe. We had no money, no contacts, and very little knowledge, but we went anyway and had a ball.

2. Examine why this accomplishment makes you satisfied or proud. Write your thoughts below each accomplishment.

Example:

1. I was able to convince my friends to spend a great amount of effort and time on a project I had conceived.
2. I had to do extensive research, planning, and coordinating just to get things off the ground.
3. It was a courageous thing to do.
4. I managed to get along in many different countries that had customs and language very different from those of the U.S.
5. We survived for six months on practically no money. I came up with a few ingenious ways to save cash.
6. The five of us got along great for the entire six months despite close quarters, differing agendas, and dissimilar personalities.
7. It was a long-term project that I stuck with despite a lack of support and other problems.
8. I learned to deal with foreign currency and various rates of exchange.

3. Filter out the skills.

Examine each numbered statement to discern the skills involved. Include even those skills that seem obvious or simple. List the skills on a separate sheet of paper.

Don't Overlook Basic Skills Many people who are assessing their skills overlook the most basic ones because they figure everyone has them and they are not worth listing. Remember that not everyone can do what you can do. Take care to include all skills.

Example:

1. (Convinced my friends): Persuasion, tenacity, salesmanship, motivation, enthusiasm, ability to motivate others
2. (Planned details of the trip): Ability to conduct research, plan, coordinate, and arrange; organization skills
3. (Did it even though I was a little bit afraid): Courage, risk-taking, boldness, self-confidence
4. (Adjusted to new customs): Adaptability, flexibility, ability to learn
5. (Survived six months on a tiny budget): Ability to manage a budget, economical, conservative
6. (Maintained friendships): Ability to compromise, respectful of friendships, outgoing, get along well with others
7. (Stuck with long-term project): Determination, focus, drive, tenacity, vision, persistence, self-confidence
8. (Learned foreign currency): Attention to detail; knowledge of exchange rates

Easily, the backpacking trip accomplishment involves well over 30 deep-seated intuitive skills that are vital to success in any professional position. These are the types of skills that interviewers will be looking for. In completing this exercise, you are preparing yourself with a list of your skills ready for the asking. And you have in hand more than a list of words—you have organized the proof (the accomplishments themselves) behind the words!

4. IDENTIFY YOUR MOST PREDOMINANT SKILLS.

As you complete this exercise, some skills reappear under almost every accomplishment you list. This frequent occurrence is an indication that the particular skill is a very strong part of your skill set. Write these predominant skills on a separate list and keep them in mind for the interview to answer such questions as, "What is your greatest strength?" or "What makes you different from the other candidates?"

You will be referring to your list of skills several times throughout this book. It will become a vital part of your marketing plan as you prepare to sell *yourself,* the product, in a job interview.

SUMMARY

In this lesson you learned why you should become familiar with your unique accomplishments and with the skills you have to offer and how this familiarity applies to the job interview. You also learned how to identify your skills using the four-step skills assessment exercise.

THE TWO-MINUTE BIO

In this lesson you learn the importance of developing and polishing a two-minute biography for use in the job interview. You draft your own personal two-minute bio using a sample bio and writing exercise.

Stop and take a few minutes to formulate a response to the invitation, "Tell me about yourself." Do it right now, out loud.

Could you easily put your background into concise highlights, or did you have to stop midway, revise your thoughts, restructure your direction, and start over and over again? Most people, while certainly the best experts on who they are, can't tell anyone else about themselves succinctly without a lot of practice and forethought.

Yet the ability to recite your background in a brief, 120-second format is vital to the job interview process. The two-minute bio offers a quick peek into your background, strengths, and career direction. Job seekers find it a useful self-introduction in a variety of situations, from the networking meeting, to casual encounters, to the job interview itself.

You will be asked to introduce yourself at the start of almost any job interview, and you will likely be asked for a brief overview of your skills. This can be a daunting start to any interview unless you are well prepared with a thoughtfully developed, practiced, and focused two-minute bio.

Guidelines to a Good Bio

While every personal bio is unique, the traditional format looks something like this:

1. Begin with a brief remark about your background, such as your schooling, hometown, or other item of interest.
2. State your most recent employer, job title, and years with the company.
3. Offer one or two sentences about your job responsibilities.
4. Mention one or two special accomplishments in your most recent positions, including skill strengths.
5. Refer to prior positions to indicate career progression.
6. Indicate career goals.

Sample Two-Minute Bios

Examine the two sample bios and note how each summarizes a lifetime in about 250 words. Focus on the organization of the information and how it flows naturally according to the guidelines above.

Experienced Marketing Manager

I was born in Argentina and moved to Cleveland with my family when I was eight years old. I graduated from Boston University with a degree in mathematics, then spent the next several years as a lieutenant in the Navy.

For the past 16 years, I have been with SENTEX, a multinational pharmaceutical company based in Cincinnati. Most recently, I was vice president of marketing and development. I managed a department of 120 marketing professionals in seven different functional specialties and a budget of $16 million. I worked hard to drive the department's productivity and competitiveness upward, and sales in the anti-infective market grew from $25 million to $230 million under my direction.

Prior to my work at SENTEX, I worked my way up from product manager to group product director with a young pharmaceutical company, ANCO, based in Detroit.

Some of the greatest strengths I've brought to my career are my ability to anticipate and analyze needs and my enthusiasm in creating a vision and a strategy to alleviate those needs. For example, in 1995, I recognized that our Field Sales Force was wasting energy and becoming unmotivated because of poor communication and an inefficient structure. I was able to revitalize the program by recommending and implementing a reorganization of Field Sales, which increased the selling effort by 40 percent.

My goals are to stay in marketing management, and I plan to keep my focus in the healthcare industry. I particularly enjoy business development and new product planning.

Aspiring Administrator

I worked my way through college to earn an Associate's degree in administration from Catonsville Community College in 1993. Despite working a full-time job and taking classes, I graduated with honors in only two years.

For the past three years, I have been with Collins and Collins, a local executive consulting firm based in Columbia, Maryland. I have acted as executive assistant to Steven Collins, a position that demands a great deal of planning, prioritizing, and flexibility. My work revolves around scheduling clients, organizing, managing, and marketing workshops, and handling mailings and customer inquiries. There has never been a dull moment, and I have enjoyed the challenges that the quick pace and encroaching deadlines always bring.

Before I joined Collins and Collins, I handled the books for Nellson Waterstreet, an accounting firm in Silver Spring. That position offered a much slower-paced atmosphere, and I enjoyed giving the work the attention to detail that it demanded.

In both of my positions, I found that I was able to develop more efficient methods of getting the job done, saving the company both time and money, and I considered that to be one of the most rewarding aspects of my career.

In my next position, I'd like the opportunity to expand on my skills in coordinating and organizing, as well as to grow a bit more into administrative management.

Avoid Irrelevant Details Don't include extraneous information. Brightest highlights only!

Creating Your Own Two-Minute Bio

Complete the following exercise to design your own two-minute bio, then practice it until it feels comfortable. Write *brief* answers to the following questions. Then arrange the information you have included into a progressive format. Keep in mind that this exercise is only a guide. Add or exclude information as your situation warrants. Just make sure the bio remains concise and takes only about two minutes to recite. Aim for approximately 250 words.

Stay Serious Avoid being "cutesy" or funny in your bio. It often backfires.

1. I was born and raised in ______________________. I attended school at ______________________ and graduated with a degree in _______________.
2. Most recently I have been working for ____________ company. My job title is/was____________________.
3. Two of my greatest strengths are _________________ and ____________.
4. I used these strengths to achieve the following special accomplishments (one or two) in my most recent position(s): ____________________________________ ____.
5. Prior to that I worked for _______________ company as ______________ (job title). There I gained a solid base in _____________________ (knowledge learned or skills used).
6. My career goals are: ____.

SUMMARY

In this lesson you learned the guidelines to writing an effective personal biography, and you used an exercise to write your own two-minute bio.

Preparing for the Interview

In this lesson you learn the important preparation techniques that enhance your confidence and self-presentation during the interview.

One challenge of the job interview is that it follows a structured game plan to which only the other team has access. The control of the situation, for the most part, is not in your hands, but in those of the other team. You have to play by the other side's rules, and you don't know exactly what those rules are until you are face to face with the interviewer.

The most stressful aspect of the interview is that it involves so many unknowns. The unknowns cause anxiety because you can't be sure that you will know how to handle them once they arise.

The best way to prepare for an interview, then, is to reduce the unknowns. This takes some work on your part, but it enables you to anticipate the possibilities and to have a game plan for how to deal with them when you need to.

Pre-Interview Preparation Techniques: Empower Yourself!

Following are the six stages to empowering yourself for an interview situation:

1. RESEARCH THE COMPANY

Many people think that researching a company before attending an interview is an *extra* step—that it is a good thing to do, but not a necessary thing to do. Wrong! These days, entering an interview with solid knowledge of the organization is vital. Why? Because interviewers today are savvy, and they are quite likely to ask you the question, "Tell us why you are interested in our company," or "What do you know about XYZ Corporation?" An answer of, "Gee, I don't know" definitely doesn't hack it. You can research a company in several ways:

- *Go to the library.* Ask the research librarian to help you locate the publications you need to find the information you want. In the reference section, you can find directories, updated quarterly, that contain company addresses, telephone numbers, names of executives, financial information, company history, affiliations, and so on. Appendix A contains a listing of such publications. You can also check back issues of trade publications and other periodicals (both local and national) for articles regarding your company of interest.
- *Go online.* Much of the information that is available in print at the library can also be found on your computer at home, saving you a trip to the library. If the company is small, local, or privately owned, however, you may find your best information at the library itself. Appendix B contains a list of online sources of company information.
- *Call the company.* Ask the company to send you its literature. You will probably receive an annual report and a brochure or two that give you some indication of corporate culture as well as financial standing, new product development, recent acquisitions, and so on.

- *Talk to people.* Never enter an interview situation without first learning all you can from people who are in the know: former company employees, friends of friends who work at the company, people who work at organizations that may do business with the company, or members of professional associations that may have key contacts. You may discover important information about your interviewer or the potential job that could make the interview process much smoother.

2. Research the Job

If you don't know for sure what the job is all about, talk to someone who does. If it is a job that is rather standard throughout the industry, such as systems analyst or accounting clerk, talk to people who have similar jobs at other companies. Ask them to tell you about what they do, and what they like and dislike about their jobs, and even what their company pay range is for that position. This enables you to do the following:

- Enter your job interview fortified with broader information about the position.
- Compare the position you may be offered to similar positions at other organizations.
- Respond knowledgeably to the interviewer's questions about your strengths and needs.

3. Know Yourself

Never enter any interview situation without first reviewing the product you are selling *(you)*. You would never think of trying to sell a vacuum cleaner to someone without first knowing what its strong points are, would you? You would be surprised how many people go to an interview without the foggiest idea how to explain what their own strengths are. Clarify your strengths in your mind before the interview so that the words come out smoothly when you need them. The interviewer will see you as prepared, confident, and well-spoken.

Make the Connection Think of your strengths in terms of what the company needs. Emphasize the strengths that the company is looking for!

Think of your strengths in terms of the contribution you can make to *that particular job* at *that particular company*. It's of no use selling the company on your ability to work independently if the current need is for someone who is a good team player. In fact, you can lose a job offer that way.

4. Know What You Want to Ask

An interview is a two-way street. Don't forget that this is the proper time for you to gather detailed information about the job you'll be doing and the company for which you'll work. It is the information you will be basing your decision on if you are made a job offer.

Never enter an interview situation without considering what information you would like to get from the interview. Ask yourself what you would like to know about the job and the company. Prepare a list to take with you in case you need to refer to it.

Come with a List It is perfectly acceptable to refer to a list of prepared questions during the interview. This makes you look organized and professional.

5. PRACTICE!

Thinking about the questions you may be asked in an interview and how you may answer them is good, but practicing them out loud is better.

You can't imagine how something sounds until you hear it out loud. Role-play interview questions and answers with a friend or spouse who can give you the feedback you need to hone your answers. Role-play two scenarios:

- Gather a list of questions that you may be asked in an interview and have your friend ask you to answer them. Ask for honest feedback. Was the answer too long, too short, too arrogant, not confident enough? Was it convincing, well presented, honest, and focused on the company's needs?
- Answer the request, "Tell me about yourself," by reciting your two-minute bio (see Lesson 3). Do this several times. Let your friend suggest improvements.

Face Your Fears Think about potential problem areas and questions you hope they *don't* ask. Prepare especially well for those, because they are likely to be brought up in the interview.

6. TAKE CARE OF DETAILS

Hundreds of little things can go wrong before and during an interview. Do not wait until the last minute to get ready for the interview. Begin as soon as you have an interview scheduled. Take these positive measures to avert any possible snags.

- Leave plenty of time to run into heavy traffic. If you end up arriving 30 minutes early, no harm done. If you end up arriving 30 minutes late, you have jeopardized the job offer.
- Bring a portable phone if you have one, the company telephone number, and the name of the person with whom you are to interview. If you run into unavoidable delays, you can call to let him or her know that you are on the way.
- Do a dry run from your home to the interview site before the actual interview date. This familiarizes you with travel time and possible parking difficulties. Bring a street or subway map if needed.
- Bring plenty of cash along in case you need to pay for parking, tolls, subway fare, and so on.
- Coordinate your interview attire well ahead of time. This way you can get your suit to the dry cleaners early, and you can run to the store to get shoe polish or a new pair of hose with plenty of time to spare.
- Place the things you want to bring in the car or by the door the evening before the interview. Double check before you leave to be sure you haven't forgotten anything.

- Make sure the car has plenty of gasoline so you don't have to fill up on the way to the interview and risk spilling gas on your suit.

WHAT TO BRING TO THE INTERVIEW

You do not want to overload your pockets, briefcase, or arms with excess objects or papers; however, empty-handed is unprepared. Assemble the following items and bring them to your interview.

- Several copies of your résumé
- A notebook with paper and a pen
- Business cards if you have them
- Cash, just in case; bring coins in case you meet a parking meter
- Your list of questions
- The phone number of the company and name of the interviewer
- A map if needed
- A portable phone
- Other papers that may be of interest to the interviewer, such as reports, sales figures, newspaper clippings, art samples, references, and so on

SUMMARY

In this lesson you learned how to anticipate possible interview snags and prepare for a winning interview.

LESSON 5

Types of Interviews

In this lesson you learn the different stages of the job interview process and the purpose of each. You also learn the "codes of behavior" for different interview settings and situations.

Interviews progress through different stages much as dates do, and each has codes of behavior. On a first date, the two parties are less familiar with each other, and each is polite and perhaps particularly reserved. The date might conclude with a peck on the cheek and a promise of a future phone call. The second date might be more relaxed. The couple might enjoy quiet time at home rather than going out on the town, and each person may feel less reserved as familiarity with the other increases. And so it progresses, as each continues to learn about the other and forms opinions about shared values and interests.

Job interviews are a slightly different version of the same process. While love and lifelong togetherness aren't being considered, the process still involves two parties assessing each other for a long-term commitment. Each is forming an opinion of the other; values, interests, talents, and personality are being explored. And the interview process progresses through levels of familiarity just like the dating game.

The Three Levels of Interviews

The interview process generally progresses through three levels of interviews.

1. The Screening Interview

The first interview is the *screening* interview. Its purpose is to weed out applicants who do not meet the basic skill requirements for a position. You are especially likely to encounter a screening interview if you respond to an ad in the newspaper.

The screening interview may be skipped if there is a mutual connection or some prior interaction between the job applicant and the company doing the hiring. In this case, the company already knows you have the basic qualifications for the job, so it doesn't need to screen your skills base.

If you encounter a screening interview, fine-tune your performance by paying attention to these tips:

- The purpose of the screening interview is to screen you *out*. Be careful not to reveal any negatives.

Keep it Serious Don't be overly chatty, funny, or indecisive during a screening interview. Remain poised and keep your answers short and direct.

- The screening interview focuses on your basic skill levels, rather than your personality characteristics. Be positive and confident about your ability to do the job.

- The screening interview often takes place over the telephone. Be prepared! Keep the materials you may need close to the phone.

Caught Off Guard! If the telephone interview catches you off guard, tell the caller you are "in the middle of a project" and ask if you can call back at a specific time later in the day.

- Screen interviews are often conducted by the human resources department. Write down the name of the interviewer. If the interview takes place in person, write a thank-you note.
- Tell the screener you are interested in the job, if you are. Show your enthusiasm.
- Don't forget to ask about the next step in the interview process.

2. The Hiring Interview

The next interview level takes place after the screening interviews have reduced the number of job candidates. If the hiring company put an employment ad in the paper, these numbers may have been reduced from about 400 respondents to maybe 6 to 8 job candidates (depending upon the number of jobs to be filled and the level of the position).

The purpose of the hiring interview is to ensure that the candidate is a right fit for the company and for the position being filled. The focus is no longer on screening you *out*, but on screening you *in*.

Here are some tips on keeping yourself in the running:

- The hiring interview is usually conducted by the manager with whom you would be working. Now is the time to let your personality shine!
- Recognize that if you have made it this far, you are probably one of the chosen few candidates. Tell the interviewer more than just the information on your résumé.
- The focus of the hiring interview is on your unique skills, experience, management style, and so on. The company is already convinced that you have the knowledge to do the job—now show how well your personality, motivation, and skills fit with the company's needs.

Stay Positive Don't let your guard down. Even though you have come back for a second interview, don't let familiarity breed stupidity. Keep your negatives to yourself!

- A thank-you note is absolutely vital. Check spelling and grammar. (See Lesson 16 for sample thank-you notes.)

3. The Confirmation Interview

The confirmation interview takes place after you have been identified as the leading candidate by the department or manager for whom you would work. This interview is conducted by the boss's boss. Essentially, the big boss is giving his or her stamp of approval on a decision that has already been made.

Follow these guidelines to survive this level of interview:

- Unless the big boss starts to ask specific skill-related questions, there is no need to try to prove your qualifications for the job. He or she is not in this to disprove your credibility; he or she simply wants to get a good feeling about you.
- Spend time building rapport. The big boss is more concerned with your motivated abilities such as attitude and good judgment. If the two of you have similar interests, let the conversation go there.

Get In and Get Out Do not try to extend the interview time to score points with the big boss. The longer you are in there, the greater the chance for something to go wrong.

- Express enthusiasm and interest in the position. Key in on the needs of the firm and your ideas and strategies regarding those needs.

Send a Thank-You Note No matter how brief the interview may be, send the big boss a thank-you note. Express respect for the company you hope to be joining.

SUMMARY

In this lesson you learned the three progressive levels of the job interview and how to handle each level of interview with finesse.

LESSON 6

Alternative Interview Formats

In this lesson you learn how to adapt to various interview settings and circumstances with confidence and composure.

Most job interviews take place in an office somewhere on the premises of the hiring company. The entire encounter is focused on a traditional structure of questions and answers in a conventional office setting.

But interviews often take place under circumstances far different from the customary one-on-one office setting. Each situation calls for a set of behaviors appropriate to the particular interview circumstances.

The Telephone Interview

An interview can take place over the telephone for a variety of reasons. The company may be located at a distance from the job applicant, or perhaps the applicant or hiring manager is out of town. Or the interview may be a basic screening call, with a set of rote questions being asked to determine fundamental qualifications.

Whatever the situation, follow these simple rules to handle a telephone interview wisely:

- Do not go ahead with the interview if you are not prepared. Make arrangements to call back at a later time that same day.
- Do not try to give an interview with the children screaming, the dog barking, or the television on in the background. Set yourself up in a quiet space or call back later.
- If you are expecting potential employers to call your home, you may want to change that silly answering machine message to one that sounds more professional. Keep it brief and do not play music or permit any background noises. Try something like, "You have reached 555-1111. Please leave a message, and we'll return your call as soon as possible. Thank you."
- Because the interviewer can't see you, it is more difficult to establish rapport over the telephone. Try to arrange a face-to-face meeting as the next step.

Choose Face-to-Face If you are given the choice between a telephone interview and a personal meeting, go for the personal meeting. You are much more likely to establish a relationship and impress the interviewer in person.

- With today's technology, telephone interviews may include conference calls with several interviewers participating at one time. This can be confusing. It is perfectly acceptable to ask that a question be repeated or to ask who is speaking. Make sure to write down the names of all participants at the beginning of the call and refer to them by name throughout the interview.

Be Energetic Keep your voice level up and your energy level high. A quiet, monotonous voice can come across the telephone line as bored, tired, or uninterested.

- Listen very carefully at the beginning of the phone conversation to get the caller's correct name and job title. You may need to refer to it later. If you don't catch it the first time around, ask the caller politely to repeat his or her name. Say something like, "I'm very glad to hear from you. I have been hoping XYZ Company would call. But I'm sorry, I didn't catch your name. Could you repeat it please?"
- As with any interview, write a thank-you note to the caller. A well written thank-you note can never hurt and can be the deciding factor on who gets the job.

THE STRESS INTERVIEW

A current trend in interviewing is to put the job candidate through a highly stressful interview situation so that his reaction to stress can be observed. The interviewer might suddenly adopt a cynical, abusive tone, and fire tough questions at the candidate. Most applicants leave the stress interview with the impression that the interviewer didn't trust or like them.

You can be assured that it's nothing personal. The interviewer is merely evaluating your ability to handle stress.

If you encounter one of these stress interview situations, remember these tips:

- Ask yourself if you want to work for an organization that asks its job candidates to endure such pressure. If the company wants to see your reaction to stress, it probably means that the job you are applying for is very stressful. Do you thrive on stress or avoid it?
- Keep calm and don't get offended. The interviewers are purposefully trying to agitate you. Realize that it is a game, and play it cool.

Keep the Vault Locked Don't give any information you weren't intending to give. The interviewer is trying to break down your defenses through the element of surprise.

- Don't give wishy-washy answers. Express 100 percent conviction in your ability to do the job. If the interviewer perceives that he is eroding your confidence, you have lost points.
- If the interview tactic succeeds in offending you so much that you decide on the spot that you would never accept a position with that organization, don't reveal your feelings during the interview. Stick it out to the end, then turn down the offer if you get one. It never pays to throw an interview, even if you know you don't want the job. The company could become useful to you later.

THE PANEL INTERVIEW

Before you receive a job offer in today's employment arena, you will more than likely have to endure a job interview that pits you against several interviewers simultaneously. This might occur in an office or conference room, with your chair facing a line of others. Or you may be escorted from office to office in an effort to introduce you to the people with whom you would work (which gives them a chance to evaluate you, no matter how brief the encounter might be).

To survive a panel interview, follow these codes of behavior:

- Keep your cool. It feels as if they've ganged up against you, but they haven't. In fact, this can be a superb opportunity to impress everyone with your savvy and poise. They'll admire your composure and fortitude.
- Answer one question at a time and place equal importance on all questions asked.

Assume Everyone Is Important Never assume that a person is unimportant or has little say in the hiring decision. That soft-spoken, innocuous person sitting quietly in the back could be your interviewer's boss!

- Pay careful attention during the introductions. When answering a question, address by name the person who asked you the question.
- If you meet several people individually, offer each person a firm handshake. If they are future colleagues, ask them to tell you a bit about their jobs. Try to get a big picture of how the divisions or

projects fit together and a feel for the corporate culture. Ask for their business cards before you leave their offices.

- Be friendly and charming, but also succinct. Rambling is deadly during a panel interview.
- It is difficult to establish rapport during a panel interview because it is a group setting. Be especially aware of maintaining good eye contact with each person in the group.

The Interview Is a Window into the Company Remember to use the interview as an opportunity to evaluate the position and the company itself. Panel interviews offer you the best insight into the way an organization is run.

- At the conclusion of the interview, ask what the next step is and express interest in the position.
- Be sure to remember everyone who participated in the interview process. Flatter them by sending each one a thank-you note afterwards.

Make Thank-You Notes Unique When writing thank-you notes to several people in the same organization, be sure to make each note unique. Include references to their particular questions, interests, or projects if you can.

The Interview with a Meal

Occasionally, an interviewer suggests that the interview take place during a breakfast, lunch, or dinner meal. This is generally a positive sign, since an interviewer only spends this much time with the strongest candidates.

While it has the outward appearance of being a more relaxed and casual encounter than the typical job interview, in fact the meal interview can be quite harrowing for the applicant. Errors such as spilled drinks and badly timed interruptions can easily occur.

Remember to follow these guidelines for a smoother mealtime interview:

- Remind yourself that the *interviewer* is having a nice meal. *You* are interviewing for a job. The meal is entirely secondary.
- Don't order anything messy. Tough-to-eat items such as French onion soup and spaghetti are no-nos.
- Don't order dessert unless the interviewer does first.
- Don't order an alcoholic beverage, even if your interviewer does.
- Don't smoke.
- Don't order the most expensive thing on the menu.

You're Not There to Eat Order something simple and light that is not hugely appetizing to you. Your food should not distract you from the task at hand.

- Don't summon the waiter or send back your food. If your drink runs dry or your food is overcooked, too bad. *You are there to be interviewed.*
- Follow the rules of etiquette. Put your napkin in your lap, and don't put your elbows on the table. You never know what might offend your interviewer.
- Let the interviewer pay the check. The one who set up the interview and suggested the meal should pay the bill.
- Keep the thank-you note focused on the interview rather than the meal. You might make small reference to the meal, such as, "Thank you for the interview on Tuesday at the Maisonette. I enjoyed learning about your background in electronics and the planned direction of XYZ Corp."

SUMMARY

In this lesson you learned about the different types of interview situations and the codes of behavior to follow for a successful interview in each setting.

LESSON 7

What Hiring Managers Look For

In this lesson you learn what interviewers are looking for when trying to fill a job vacancy and how to use this knowledge to interview successfully.

The job interview is one of the most anxiety-producing situations one can encounter. We are expected to walk blindly into an unknown office setting, impress a number of people with whom we are unacquainted, be on our very best behavior throughout a stressful and uncomfortable period of time, and anticipate the events of an entirely unfamiliar situation.

It is true that the burden of stress is on the interviewee rather than the interviewer. After all, the interviewer has all the advantages. She is the one who chooses the time and place of the meeting. She is the one with the job description in front of her, and the list of qualifications and skills she hopes to find for the job. And, of course, she has the power to make the hiring choice.

Wouldn't the whole interviewing process be easier if the job candidate could somehow take a peek at the interviewer's game plan before the job interview? Couldn't you play the interview game much more adeptly if you somehow knew what was being sought in a job candidate before the interview began? Maybe the interviewer's game plan isn't as mysterious as you think.

EVALUATING JOB CANDIDATES

Hiring managers typically evaluate a job candidate along two broad dimensions.

Job Expertise A job candidate's level of knowledge, skills, industry-related experience, and technical expertise as it relates to the job at hand.

Personal Skills A candidate's unique set of personal behaviors and values, which allow him to achieve success in the particular position to be filled.

While most people assume that hiring managers place strong emphasis on a job candidate's level of experience (job expertise), in reality, it is the personal skills that hold the most weight in the hiring decision.

Focus on Your Achievements Don't undersell your personal skills in the job interview. Use illustrations of past achievements to highlight positive personal qualities.

While technical skills, job-related knowledge, and prior job experience are certainly a vital part of any hiring decision, the overriding criterion in the decision is whether or not the job candidate's personality characteristics are consistent with successful job performance. After all, it is generally easy to teach a motivated and honest person to become successful in many job functions, but it is quite difficult to teach an unmotivated and dishonest person to be successful at anything. Hiring managers figure that they can teach technical skills much more easily than they can teach new behaviors.

The Eight Personal Qualities Hiring Managers Look for Most

There really is no mystery as to what hiring managers would like to see in the job candidates they are interviewing. The applicant who shows these personal qualities along with job skills is every manager's ideal.

1. Willingness to Learn

Any job interviewer worth his salt will assess you for your interest in learning new skills and for your enthusiasm for doing things according to the specific values and direction of the company.

What to Do in the Interview: Don't go into the interview with the goal of convincing them that you already know everything you need to know to be a success on the job or that you've seen it all before. The interviewer would prefer to think you have a bit of room to grow...into the company's way of doing business.

2. Motivation

Every employer, whether hiring a custodian, school teacher, nurse, or executive, needs an employee who is motivated—someone who accepts challenges and who is not a quitter; someone who is dedicated enough to put time and energy into important projects and who works hard to do the best job possible.

What to Do in the Interview: Use stories of past accomplishments to illustrate times that you have been challenged and have succeeded at difficult tasks. Steer clear of overemphasizing your busy life outside of the workplace. You do not want the interviewer to fear a lack of dedication to your job.

3. Integrity

Why would an employer hire someone she can't trust? No matter how good you might be at your job, you are of no use to any employer if you are not honest and loyal.

What to Do in the Interview: Make sure you do not convey any negative information about your past or current employer. And, of course, keep all classified information regarding previous projects to yourself. You will gain respect and admiration (and maybe even a job) because of your moral character.

4. Communication Skills

It is important not only that you know how to read and write well, but that you can convey important information to others in a clear and concise manner. Can you keep others apprised of situations and information so that projects run smoothly and the process is efficient?

What to Do in the Interview: Use direct illustrations of past communication victories. Have you ever made a project run more efficiently because you established better communication channels? Have you ever revised communication procedures to increase information flow? A careful communicator is an important asset at any level.

5. Ability to Get Along with Others

The interviewer will assess whether you are a team player, an individualist, a maverick, or a loose cannon. Employers tend to look for the worker who can toe the company line when needed and who gives in to the interests of the group when necessary, but someone who can hold on to his principles and ideas when the going gets tough. Generally, employers want someone who makes noteworthy contributions to the company but doesn't make waves.

What to Do in the Interview: Don't overemphasize your nonconformist side. You don't want to be seen as a renegade. If you tell a story of a time that you succeeded on a project because you stood your ground against the crowd, make sure to include a lot of praise and statements of respect for the others involved in the project.

6. Positive Attitude

Nobody wants to work with a whiner. Complaining, tattling, undercutting, and gossiping are all behaviors that undermine productivity and have caused managers countless headaches over the centuries. Employers want to bring on board someone who gets along with fellow workers and who pitches in when needed.

What to Do in the Interview: Never complain about a previous job or boss, even if directly asked to do so in the interview. (You might get questions such as, "Tell me about the worst boss you ever had," or "What did you like least about your last position?") The more positive things you have to say about people and projects you have encountered, the more positively you will be evaluated.

Also, don't balk if the interviewer asks if you'd be willing to do a task you consider demeaning, such as making coffee for the boss. The interviewer is probably just checking your attitude. Smile and ask if the boss likes cream and sugar.

7. PERSONAL CHEMISTRY

Employers hire people with whom they'd like to work. Perhaps it is unfair that the guy who is a wonder with a softball glove gets hired just because the hiring manager happens to be the company team coach. It is difficult, however, to remove the impact that personal chemistry and rapport have on the hiring decision. And, after all, personality is a legitimate factor in the hiring decision. An employer figures that someone who gets along with her and with other members of the staff will be a productive part of the team.

What to Do in the Interview: It's tough to coach someone on how to be likeable. Some people exude great personal charisma in interview settings, while others let situational stress or shyness override their charm. Do your best to establish rapport with the interviewer. It is okay to stray off the immediate professional topic a bit during the interview, just don't overdo it.

Let the Interviewer Set the Topic Keep the interview professional, but friendly. Go ahead and talk sports, music, and so on, but only if a logical opening for casual conversation appears or if the interviewer brings the subject up first.

8. CONFIDENCE

An interviewer looks for a candidate with a strong but realistic level of confidence. Overconfidence paves the way to expensive failures. Under-confidence leads to lack of productivity.

What to Do in the Interview: Be neither boastful nor self-effacing. Never pretend you can solve all the company's problems in an hour, and never admit that the company's problems sound overwhelming to you. Project self-assurance, level-headedness, and poise.

COMPANY BAGGAGE

For several reasons, it can be helpful to know what goes into a hiring decision. First, it can help you to handle the curve balls that can sometimes be hurled at you during the interview. Second, it can ease the feeling of rejection to know that occasionally, interview situations have prearranged circumstances which, although beyond your control, have played a big part in determining the outcome of the selection process. And third, it can help you ask the right questions to determine the interviewer's mindset, so that you can play the interview game with finesse.

Interviewers and the companies they represent may inflict baggage on the hiring process which shifts the direction of the interview dramatically:

1. **The Other Guy.** The hiring managers may be looking for anyone who is as far removed as possible from the last worker they had in the position. That worker may have been too quiet, or too talkative, or too assertive, or not assertive enough, and because of that trait, the company experienced a problem that it is now trying to repair.

Solution: Ask about the strengths and weaknesses of the person who previously held the position for which you are interviewing. This gives you a chance to emphasize the parts of your personality the company likes and steer clear of those that are frowned on.

2. **Indecision.** The company may not be too sure what it is looking for. Sometimes managers need a jack-of-all-trades and have failed to narrow the job description sufficiently.

   Solution: Ask for a clear description of the position early in the interview. If the interviewer tends to remain unfocused, ask him to clarify the most vital parts of the job and emphasize those when describing your strengths.

3. **A Busy Schedule.** Once in a while you may find yourself in an interview situation in which you feel that you are imposing on the interviewer just by being there. She seems busy and distracted and quite uninterested in the whole process.

   Solution: Remain polite and focused. Ignore the interruptions and accept any apologies graciously. Move the interview into a more positive direction by asking at the end of the interview if there might be anyone else connected with the job whom you could meet.

4. **A Targeted Candidate.** Your interview may be only an obligation that the interviewer is fulfilling while in fact the position has already been unofficially filled by someone else.

Solution: If you feel this may be the case, continue with the interview and give it your best. You never know what may happen down the road. Perhaps the pre-chosen candidate will drop out of the picture. Shoot for that back-up spot just in case.

SUMMARY

In this lesson you learned about the interview process from the hiring manager's perspective and you learned several strategies to help you convey the qualities the hiring managers are looking for. You also learned solutions to troublesome interview situations.

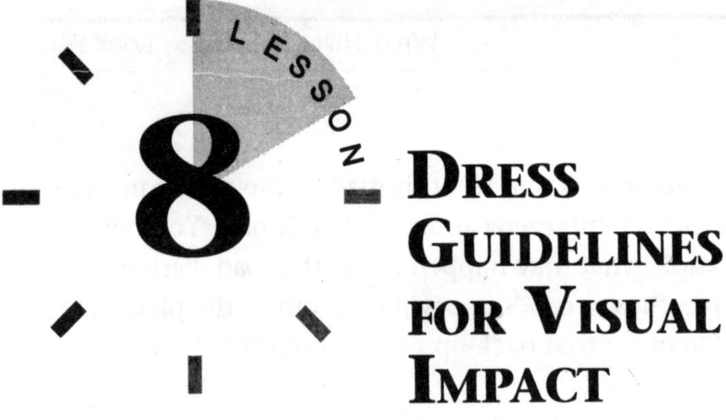

Dress Guidelines for Visual Impact

In this lesson you learn how to look professional in an interview by the clothes you wear and the image you convey.

Put yourself in the place of an interviewer for the moment. Pretend that you want to hire someone terrific for a position as, say, an office manager. You want someone who is professional, motivated, and intelligent. In the interviews, you will assess all candidates' qualities based upon three things:

- The way they look
- The way they speak
- What they say

This "image," the way a person looks and speaks, can make up a whopping two-thirds of the hiring decision. It is therefore vital to give your outward appearance the attention and polish that is necessary to convey your best professional qualities.

How to Look Your Best for an Interview

Your first reaction to this lesson may be, "But I already know how to dress. I've been dressing myself for years now!"

It is important to recognize, however, that the occasion for which you must concentrate so much fashion energy is one with which you probably do not have much experience: A job interview is unlike any other situation for which you dress. In few other social or business settings are you judged so profoundly on the way you present yourself.

At your interview, you will strive to convey the image of a professional, dynamic, hard-working, responsible person. For most interview situations, this means a conservative and traditional look. Do not attempt to make any other type of statement with your clothing, unless you want to express some originality for an interview in an industry that thrives on creativity, such as fashion or advertising.

TIPS FOR A POLISHED LOOK

The impression that you want to convey is that you care about your appearance, but not that your appearance is all that you care about. Cleanliness counts. Neatness counts. Good taste counts.

- A woman should wear a neat, tailored hairstyle. If your hair is longer than shoulder length, consider pulling it back for a sharper look.

How Much Makeup? Women should apply makeup with a light touch. A natural look is much better than the "overdone" look. You want to look pleasant, but not glamorous.

- A beard can impart either a rugged look or an intellectual look. While facial hair might not be right for all interview situations, it is acceptable to sport a well-groomed mustache or beard in today's business climate.

- Women's fingernails should be clean, neat, and understated. Stay away from flashy colors and designs.
- Men must pay attention to their hands. Hands should be clean, with trimmed, neat nails.

DRESS GUIDELINES FOR MEN

The business world tends to think of itself as a conservative environment. You must appear at your interview dressed to conform to that conservative image. Once you are hired, you can dress to blend in with the actual practice of the specific workplace.

- Wear a suit of charcoal to light gray or a dark, muted navy blue. Browns, and especially beiges, make a much weaker presentation. A solid black suit, on the other hand, is overpowering. Don't go near the polyester materials; they look cheap and make you appear unsuccessful. Watch out also for the out-of-date bold pinstripes or bold solid colors. Remember: dark, wool, muted, traditional.
- Your shirt should be white and traditionally tailored (no collarless or collar-of-another-color shirts, please). A pale-blue or cream-colored shirt is a distant second choice. The shirt must be crisp and fresh to accent your professional, no-nonsense attitude.

No Short Sleeves The shirt you wear must have long sleeves, even in the summer months. No excuses. Short sleeves will greatly diminish your professional look.

- Choose a tie that does not scream for attention. A stripe, foulard, or paisley print in colors that complement your suit is a smart choice. A solid tie is fine, as long as it complements the suit and is an acceptable width (about the same width as the lapels on your suit). Steer clear of ties that are too casual, such as linen or wool, and ties that have bold patterns, pictures, or colors. Bow ties and string ties are forbidden.

The Tie Isn't Optional You absolutely must wear a tie to an interview, even if the people who work there do not. Wearing one makes the statement that you are serious about wanting to work there and are willing to "spruce yourself up" to prove it.

- Keep your shoes on the conservative side: either black or brown wing tips or other lace-up style dress shoes. Don't try to get away with a shoe that is too casual; it can easily ruin your whole look.
- Choose a belt that matches your shoes. Keep the style dressy and conservative with a subdued buckle.
- Your socks should be appropriate for your suit, that is, blue, black, or gray: no bold patterns or casual styles, please. You have better things to draw attention to in the interview than your socks.

Longer Socks Are Better Over-the-calf socks are best since your leg won't peek out in the gap between pants leg and sock top when you sit down or cross your legs, and they're less likely to fall down and gather around your ankles.

- Steer clear of excessive jewelry. Never wear earrings (or nose rings), chains, bracelets, fraternity rings, or class rings. Cuff links are acceptable if you wear French cuffs, but they should be subtle, not flashy.

The Two "W"s The only jewelry appropriate for males to wear to an interview are the two "W"s: the *wedding band* and the *watch.*

- The watch you wear to an interview should be tasteful and professional. Leave the heavy sports model at home. A traditional leather-strap model is a good choice.
- Briefcases come in many styles these days. Choose one that you are comfortable with. A plain black, brown, or burgundy is best. Take care that it is not overly worn and shabby.

DRESS GUIDELINES FOR WOMEN

A professional suit is the best bet for a woman on a job interview, no matter what the level of job. Although acceptable styles and colors vary more for women than for men, follow these general suggestions:

- Choose a style with a flattering but professional fit. No short skirts or skin-tight styles.
- Steer clear of overly bold suit patterns or colors. You want to look serious and professional, not flighty and unmanageable.

- Solids, muted plaids, and pinstripes are all acceptable interviewing attire. The best colors to stick with are grays, navy, and black.
- Your blouse should be simple rather than flashy, and its color should be subtle and professional. A crisp, white blouse is safe and looks sharp with everything.

Don't Show Too Much Never wear a blouse that is low-cut, sleeveless, see-through, or provocative in any way. You want to land a job, not a date.

- Avoid jewelry that draws attention to itself. It should add accent to your overall look, rather than dominate it.
- A string of pearls or a delicate chain is appropriate neckwear for a woman on an interview. Pins are acceptable and can look professional, yet at the same time add a bit of panache to an outfit (and may even be a conversation piece). A well-tied scarf can achieve the same result, but beware of garish patterns.
- Earrings should be small and subtle. No large hoops or dangles.

Avoid Making a Statement Do not allow your jewelry to make political or religious statements for you! Leave all "telltale" jewelry at home.

- Shoes should be of the classic pump style, with closed heel and toe in solid, dark colors only, please. The heel should be no more than 1-1/2" high. Stray from these suggestions and your shoes will severely weaken your professional statement.

Shoes Are Important Too Be sure that your shoes are well-polished and not worn at the heels. You can get away with scuffed shoes when sitting at a desk crunching numbers all day, but in an interview your shoes will be noticed. An interviewer might infer from shabby shoes that you are careless, unprofessional, or not detail-oriented.

- Pantyhose should not draw attention to themselves. They should be of neutral skin tones only!
- Do not carry a purse into the interview. Attempting to juggle both purse and briefcase can be awkward. Put "purse items" into a briefcase pocket.
- You may carry a briefcase of black, brown, or burgundy with traditional styling. A shoulder strap is fine, although carrying a briefcase by its handle has a more authoritative look.

SUMMARY

In this lesson you learned simple guidelines to polishing your appearance and creating a professional, tailored image for the job interview.

LESSON 9

Projecting Success

In this lesson you learn simple strategies for presenting yourself in an interview setting as a competent, savvy business professional.

The Professional Image

While it isn't realistic to attempt to recreate your personal image overnight, it's certainly wise to take the time to add some polish and panache to your business behaviors before setting foot in an interviewer's office.

A large part of presenting yourself as a responsible business person is your conduct during the interview. Let's walk through a typical job interview scenario and address some ideas you can use to make the interview run more smoothly.

Many qualities factor into the professional, business-savvy image you want to create: etiquette, enthusiasm, courtesy, and simple common sense.

Personal Preparation Before the Interview

You have prepared a catalog of your credentials, formulated answers to tough questions, and chosen the appropriate wardrobe for your interview. Be sure to prepare your person as well.

- Don't sabotage a potentially great interview performance with poor hygiene. Since interviews tend to be sweaty situations, a thorough shower, shampoo, and shave on the day of the interview are highly recommended.
- Be aware of good oral hygiene on the interview day. Use mouthwash at home, and take a breath freshener or breath mints in the car with you to pop into your mouth when you arrive.
- If a haircut is due, schedule time to make it happen before the interview.

Lose the Scent Avoid using perfume or after-shave. The interviewer may be allergic or sensitive to overpowering scents.

- Throw your chewing gum in the trash before walking into the building. Chewing gum in an interview appears sloppy.
- Don't smoke a cigarette in your car or outside of the building just prior to the interview. It leaves a telltale unpleasant odor on your clothes and in your hair.

PROJECTING SUCCESS: THE BEGINNING OF THE INTERVIEW

The interview begins when you walk into the front door of the building. Be alert to the impression you are making on everyone you meet.

- While waiting for the interview to begin, be pleasant and courteous to the receptionist. Do not interrupt his or her work with copious small talk, but a few cordial comments can't hurt. You might stick with something totally noncommittal, such as the weather, or a completely inoffensive remark, such as, "What a panoramic view you have from the lobby!"

Only a Few Words Keep the small talk to a very basic level. Do not get into any political or religious discussions with the receptionist, and under no circumstances should you make observations about the company or about the way he or she looks.

- Be alert and responsive from the moment you arrive in the building. Smile at everyone who passes you in the lobby. Your potential co-workers may be checking you out incognito.
- When meeting the interviewer for the first time (perhaps you have been waiting in the lobby area), stand and shake his or her hand. Do not remain sitting unless specifically asked to do so. Standing to shake hands shows alertness and enthusiasm.
- Allow the interviewer to initiate the handshake. Make yours firm and friendly, not weak and wimpy or overly aggressive. You may appear domineering if you extend your hand first.
- Don't wear a coat if the weather is at all bearable. This saves the awkward "coat shuffle" when you arrive, and it avoids the embarrassing possibility of forgetting it on your way out the door.
- Allow the interviewer to lead the way back to the office or conference room in which the interview will take place. Walk confidently: Stand up straight and do not hesitate.

- Don't sit down in the interviewer's office until a seat is offered! This is merely common courtesy. You might ask, "Where would you like me to sit?"
- Accept a cup of coffee if it is offered. This is a good idea even if you aren't a coffee drinker. It will set the mood of the interview on a more casual and relaxed level. But...
- Don't ask for a coffee refill or for cream and sugar unless they are initially offered. (In other words, don't make the interviewer get back up or go back to the coffee room after he (or she) has already fetched your coffee for you.) The same holds true if the interviewer has had someone else bring the coffee. If you don't like it black, too bad. You are there to be interviewed, not to enjoy a cup of coffee. Also...
- Don't request alternative beverages such as tea, juice, or water. If the interviewer asks, "Would you like a cup of coffee?" you should reply, "Coffee sounds great, thanks." If you don't like coffee, you never even have to take a sip.

Leave Your Briefcase on the Floor *Do not* put your briefcase on the desk or table when you sit down. It should lean against your chair or a nearby wall.

- Don't make any reference to the interviewer's (or anyone else's) appearance. Greeting someone with, "Boy, are you tall!" or "You are younger than you sounded on the phone," is completely inappropriate. Even positive comments, such as, "I like your jacket," or "Nice tie," are not a good idea.

PROJECTING SUCCESS: THE MIDDLE OF THE INTERVIEW

Your answers to the interviewer's questions are important, but your words do not tell the whole story about you. Watch your body language.

- Never explain that you are nervous; it makes you look as if tough situations befuddle you. If you feel that you must buy yourself time to settle your nerves before you answer a question, just say, "Let me take just a moment to give that some thought."
- Don't apologize throughout the interview for such imperfections as a sloppy résumé, torn stockings, windblown hair, or lack of a pen or pencil. If an apology is necessary, such as for a late arrival, be brief but sincere and don't bring the subject up again. Too many apologies make you appear weak.
- Don't perch on the edge of your chair or lean on the interviewer's desk. On the other hand, don't slouch so deeply into your chair that you look as if you're ready for a nap. Sit comfortably with your back against the back of the chair to look relaxed yet attentive.

No Laughing *Don't* giggle or laugh nervously. Keep the extraneous sounds to a minimum so that when you have something to say it has more impact.

- Don't fold your hands behind your head and lean back in the chair. This appears pompous.
- Keep your legs still! Don't bounce your knees up and down or continually shift crossed legs. It's best to keep both feet solidly planted on the floor through most of

the interview. An occasional cross at the knee or ankle is fine as long as it does not distract the interviewer.

- Keep your hands quiet during the interview. Either hold a pen or pencil (don't tap it!) or keep your hands folded on your lap. Your hands reveal your nervousness if they linger around your face, pull at your hair, tap upon the table, or make other extraneous movements. You may, of course, gesture naturally with them when speaking or making a point.
- Let your face break into a smile now and then. Job hunters are sometimes afraid that smiling makes them appear unprofessional or lightweight, but in reality, just the opposite is true. The interviewer sees you as relaxed, friendly, and comfortable in a business setting if you are able to smile.
- Show interest in what the interviewer is saying. Respond with smiles, nodding your head, and small verbal affirmations such as, "I see," or "That sounds interesting."
- Maintain good eye contact with the interviewer. Resist the temptation to look down at your hands, out the window, or out the open office door. Allow rapport to build and accentuate your listening skills.
- Don't "close up" by folding your arms or clutching your briefcase across your chest.
- Don't look at your watch or at the clock on the wall. It makes you look as if you feel there is something more important than your job interview.

PROJECTING SUCCESS: THE END OF THE INTERVIEW

The interview ends when you walk out the front door of the building. Be gracious to everyone on your way out.

- Allow the interviewer to close the interview. It is not up to you to decide when the interview is over.
- When the interviewer stands up at the close of the interview, that is a signal that you should stand too. He will probably then begin to usher you to the door.
- You may initiate the handshake that occurs at the end of the interview. Express thanks for the interviewer's time and your interest in the position.
- Say good-bye to all participants in the interview process who are still the room when the interview is over.
- Maintain your confidence and composure until you are well out of the building. Never reveal that you found the situation stressful.
- You may engage in small talk at the end of the interview. If it seems appropriate, you might ask about something in the interviewer's office that could spark a conversation, such as pictures, trophies, or knick-knacks.

These suggestions offer powerful ways to make you appear confident and adept in professional situations. Try not to be too self-conscious about your own body or personal movements. You might practice a few of the basic maneuvers, such as the handshake and confident gait, but it is also important to be yourself. Within certain limits, it is better to be relaxed and natural with the interviewer than to have perfectly planned movements that look rehearsed and stilted.

SUMMARY

In this lesson you learned how to present yourself as professional and confident throughout all phases of the job interview.

Interviewing Strategies

In this lesson you learn the 14 basic do's and the 14 basic don'ts of the job interview and how to sell your skills to a potential employer through the use of examples.

What makes for a good job interview? This question is not easily answered. There are many unpredictable factors: What type of setting you'll be in; what kind of personality the interviewer has; what kind of expectations the company has at the start of the process.

But the job seeker—whether an entry-level recent graduate or a senior-level manager—can put certain aces up his or her sleeve that can ensure an impressive interview performance.

14 Rules of Thumb for the Job Interview

1. **Match Needs.** The first rule you are taught in any sales course is to keep your mouth shut about your product until you discern the needs of the customer. If you can figure out a company's needs *before* you start to talk about your strengths, then you can emphasize the strengths you have that fit its needs.

Make Them Ask First Let the interviewer ask the first question. It may be something general like, "Tell me about yourself." Rather than launching into details that may be all wrong for the position, say politely: "Well, I know so little about the position you have available that I'd like to get a bit of information about that first. Then I'll be able to answer your questions with more clarity and focus."

2. **Relax.** Interviews are obviously stress-inducing. For many job seekers, relaxing, or at least *appearing* to be relaxed, is the biggest hurdle. The key is not to force it. Engage in small talk, make plenty of eye contact, and, of course, smile!

Don't Dress Casually You may be tempted to wear clothes that are comfortable and casual to help you relax. Don't do it. Your appearance must be crisp and professional no matter what the occupation or job level.

3. **Listen.** A good listener can impress an interviewer much more than a good talker can. This is because a listener will pick up the interests and character of the company and can structure answers accordingly.

Learn the Lingo Keep an ear open to names and acronyms used by the interviewer. You may need to refer to them later.

4. **Clarify.** To show that you are thinking and paying attention, clarify what the interviewer is saying by paraphrasing what has been said or summarizing your understanding of key points. This way you can show off your knowledge of the issues and your concern for the company's needs.
5. **Ask Questions.** The easiest way to kill an interview is to fail to ask questions. And don't wait to be asked if you have any before you ask them; interject them at the appropriate points throughout the interview.
6. **Express Focused Goals.** A person who knows where he is going impresses us as having confidence, intelligence, and leadership ability. You project indecisiveness and a weak, lackadaisical attitude if your goals appear vague and meandering.
7. **Be Specific.** The more specific and quantified your questions and answers, the more you convince the interviewer of your skills and accomplishments.
8. **Polish Your Facts.** Have dates and timelines clearly in mind so that your presentation shows forethought. If you can't remember a date or other detail, don't spend too much time groping for it. Lengthy pauses to search your mind for exact dates can drain the energy from your presentation.
9. **Use Notes.** It is completely acceptable to refer to notes or to your résumé during the interview. It is also fine to take notes, but don't concentrate on this so extensively that it interferes with a comfortable flow of conversation or causes you to avoid eye contact.
10. **Keep the Ball Rolling.** You appear savvy and professional if you establish a continuing relationship with the company beyond the end of the interview.

Try to schedule the time and place for the next meeting or at least discern what future plans are for the interviewing process. Ask who else you might be talking with as part of the hiring process or ask who makes the final decision and when.

Get to Know the Place Request a tour of the facilities, if appropriate, or ask to meet other members of the office or team you hope to join.

11. **Express Interest.** If two otherwise equal job candidates express differing levels of interest in the position, the one with the most enthusiasm for the position will most certainly get the job.

12. **Ask For a Business Card.** Too often a job seeker completely forgets the name of the person with whom he just interviewed and is too embarrassed to ask. You need that name and its correct spelling for future correspondence, including the thank-you note.

Get the Name Right It is wise to look for a nameplate or other indication of job title and spelling while you are in the interviewer's office.

13. **Be Flexible.** Now is not the time to stick resolutely to your guns about work schedule, job duties, or other aspects of the position. Express flexibility throughout the interview process, and become more strongly focused on your needs after you receive the offer.

14. **Stay on the Side of Respect.** It is better to avoid the use of first names unless invited. Projecting a

reserved yet friendly attitude gives an air of professionalism and level-headedness.

14 Things to Avoid in the Interview

1. **Don't Be Late.** What does tardiness convey to an employer, no matter how good the excuse? Unfortunately, the impression created is that of laziness, disorganization, thoughtlessness, self-importance, bad attitude, and lack of interest. Would *you* hire someone like that? Enough said.
2. **Don't Dominate.** Let the interviewer lead the interview. Thoughtful questions and well placed interjections are appreciated, but attempts to overpower are not.
3. **Don't Ramble.** Take care not to answer questions that were not asked. Extraneous information, especially when it comes off the top of your head and is unrehearsed, is usually detrimental to your cause.
4. **Don't Argue with the Interviewer.** There is no way to win an argument in a job interview. Pointing out the interviewer's mistakes or questioning facts about the job appears bullish and negative.

If You've Said Enough, Stay Quiet Interviewers may attempt to encourage you to continue talking by remaining silent when you have finished a thought. Don't give in to the urge to fill in the silence with additional words!

5. **Don't Use Diluted Language.** Phrases such as "and stuff," "or something," "you know," and "sort of" sound unprofessional and ineffectual. They dilute your message of confidence.

6. **Don't Use Overinflated Language.** Phrases and words such as "re," "per," and "per se" can sound hokey and out of place.

7. **Don't Bring the Kitchen Sink.** Remove unneeded papers from your briefcase before the interview so that you carry only the papers you need into the interview. This helps you avoid doing the "panic shuffle" while searching for a résumé.

8. **Don't Undersell Yourself.** Experts say that most of us find it tough to "brag" in an interview. Remember, though, that potential employers don't know you, and if you don't tell them how good you are in the interview, you'll never have a chance to prove it on the job.

9. **Don't Beep in an Interview.** Turn off all mechanical devices: cell phones, watches, beepers, etc. They are annoying and show lack of planning.

10. **Don't Interrupt.** Interrupting a person who is speaking is rude, whether you are in an interview or not. It shows lack of respect, and it makes you appear overeager and careless.

11. **Don't Mention Other Offers.** Don't attempt to make the point that you are a sought-after commodity by bringing up other interviews or offers. It creates the same effect as a boy on a date discussing his other girlfriends: He looks self-centered and disloyal.

12. **Don't Talk Money.** You want to give the impression that you are motivated by a strong work ethic,

an interest in learning, and enthusiasm for the company and the field in general. You do *not* want to sound as if you're there for the money. Let the interviewer bring up the salary issue first.

13. **Don't Ask How You Did.** Don't close the interview with "Well, how did I do?" or, "Do you think I have a chance?" It completely erodes your look of confidence.

14. **Don't Assume.** Don't let erroneous expectations about the position or the company throw you off guard. What you hear before the interview and what is conveyed during the interview may be quite different.

SUMMARY

In this lesson you learned 14 key tips for having an impressive interview and 14 important stumbling blocks.

LESSON 11

Interviewing Hazards and How to Overcome Them

In this lesson you learn 10 common potential negative factors that job seekers may sense and strategies for dealing effectively with these hazards at the interview.

Most of us enter the interviewing situation with trepidation—fear that a particular skeleton in our closet will creep out and single-handedly ruin our chances of landing the job we want. We worry that situations that are beyond our control, such as our age or bad experiences from our distant past, may act to dramatically reduce our possibilities for interviewing success.

Yet most of our so-called skeletons are not as large and looming a problem as we perceive them to be. Let's examine some potential interviewing hazards—the skeletons we fear the most—and look at productive and positive ways to address these hazards.

10 Common Interviewing Hazards

Job seekers often enter the interview feeling destined for failure because of these common negative factors:

1. "No one will want to hire me because I'm too old."

The company's concern:

- The company may worry that older workers will think rigidly, be inflexible, and be stale in their knowledge and skills.

How to overcome this in an interview:

- First, recognize that age is much less a negative hiring issue than ever before. Employers now care less about longevity and more about the extensive industry knowledge and breadth of experience that only older workers possess. And they recognize that older employees tend to be emotionally stronger and more stable than younger employees.
- In the interview, focus on alleviating the company's concerns. Demonstrate that your skills are current, your thinking is dynamic, and your enthusiasm is strong by using solid examples of recent successes. Emphasize your extensive knowledge and connections in the field, but explain that you recognize the need to continue to grow and learn.

2. "No one will want to hire me because I'm too young."

The company's concern:

- The company may worry that you have not been tested in tough situations and that you may be overwhelmed or limited in ability to produce results.

How to overcome this in an interview:

- Focus on problems that you overcame in past positions or at school, problems that involved scenarios to which the employer can relate. Demonstrate an ability to handle people with assertiveness and tact. Present yourself as goal-oriented and results-driven. Show through concrete examples that you are a quick and enthusiastic learner.

3. "NO ONE WILL WANT TO HIRE ME BECAUSE I'M UNDERQUALIFIED."

The company's concern:

- The company may worry that your experience in the field is too narrow and that you have not had a chance to prove yourself in the industry.

How to overcome this in an interview:

- Focus on the transferable skills you used in your former positions, even if the industry you are coming from is very dissimilar. For example, if you scheduled patient appointments for doctors in a medical practice, you can apply those same skills to arrange meetings and court dates for a legal firm.

Try Volunteer Work If you are changing careers, you may also want to consider doing volunteer work in the field you are attempting to break into. This gives you great networking connections and serves as wonderful proof of an enthusiastic, motivated attitude toward your career change.

4. "NO ONE WILL WANT TO HIRE ME BECAUSE I'M OVERQUALIFIED."

The company's concern:

- The company may worry that you could become bored or frustrated with the responsibilities of the job and therefore quickly leave the company—a costly proposition. Or, you may be a threat to supervisors who fear a know-it-all attitude or, worse, a threat to their own jobs. The interviewer may also be suspicious that you couldn't handle your previous higher-level responsibilities and that you may buckle under pressure.

How to overcome this in an interview:

- Convince the interviewer that the position for which you are applying is right for you *at this stage in your life and career.*

Changing Direction for a Reason If you cite increased outside responsibilities, such as a growing family, as a reason for your choosing a new career direction, be sure to emphasize that you still have strong dedication toward accepting challenges and making room for growth.

- Also, emphasize your past successes and your strong work ethic. Point out your interest in longevity and stability at this point in your career.

5. "NO ONE WILL WANT TO HIRE ME BECAUSE I'M OVERPAID."

The company's concern:

- Perhaps the salary the company can afford to pay you is lower than the salary you have made in your current or previous job, and management is afraid you will quickly leave the company in search of greener pastures.

How to overcome this in an interview:

- While this is a concern for many job seekers, it should not even surface as a problem in the job interview. Why? Because you should not be discussing salary until the job offer has been put on the table. The interviewer will not know what your current or past salary has been unless you spill the beans too soon. (See Lesson 17 for proper techniques in salary negotiation.)
- Perhaps the real problem is that you do not want to take a job that pays less than what you have been making, and you are afraid that the jobs with the salary you want are not out there. Give it a try: Most people are pleasantly surprised to find that they can at least match, and often improve upon, their most recent salaries.

6. "NO ONE WILL WANT TO HIRE ME BECAUSE I HAVE A GAP IN MY EMPLOYMENT HISTORY."

The company's concern:

- When a company sees an employment gap, it is suspicious of possible failures or problems that could resurface if you take a job with that company.

How to overcome this in an interview:

- Don't bring up the gap in employment unless you are directly asked to explain it in the job interview.
- Recognize that because of the downsizing and mergers that are taking place in the workplace today, many job seekers have gaps of time during which they were unemployed. If your unemployment was caused by such an event, explain it without being defensive. No matter what the cause of your unemployment, acknowledge the positive aspects of the experience, such as your increased networking connections and perspective on the industry or your chance to spend time taking a college course.

7. "NO ONE WILL WANT TO HIRE ME BECAUSE I'VE BEEN A JOB HOPPER."

The company's concern:

- The company may worry that it will go to the expense to bring you on board and train you, only to have you leave after a very short time.

How to overcome this in an interview:

- Keep all explanations on a positive note. Do not place blame with rotten former bosses, lack of training, broken promises, and so on. Simply explain that you have been searching for a position that will allow you increasing challenges and growth and that this company offers it. Prove, through the use of examples, how well your skills match the needs of this company. Talk about your enthusiasm for making a solid contribution to the company and your interest in maintaining stability and longevity with a solid organization.

8. "NO ONE WILL WANT TO HIRE ME BECAUSE I'VE HAD A NEGATIVE EMPLOYMENT SITUATION."

The company's concern:

- If you were fired in the past, there must have been a problem. The company is afraid that same problem will resurface while you are in its employ.

How to overcome this in an interview:

- Do not reveal any negative situations unless directly asked. If you must explain a negative situation, keep it brief and blame-free. Emphasize how you have learned from the situation and emphasize that the same problem will not reoccur.
- If you simply had a troublesome relationship with a former boss or co-workers but were not fired, there is no need to share these negative details in an interview.

9. "NO ONE WILL WANT TO HIRE ME BECAUSE I HAVEN'T HAD THE PROPER EDUCATION."

The company's concern:

- The company may worry that without schooling you won't have the basic tools needed to handle certain aspects of the job. It may also be looking for proof that you can undergo the long-term dedication necessary to achieve a degree.

How to overcome this in an interview:

- You may need to consider the importance of a degree to the position you are interested in. The need for a degree could be very real, in which case you may have to think about the possibilities of pursuing additional education.

- If you have had extensive experience in the field but simply lack the degree itself, employers are often willing to consider your experience as "equivalent" to a degree. It is your task in the interview, then, to demonstrate how your past experience directly relates to the position you want and how your real-life job background has prepared you well for new challenges.

10. "No one will want to hire me because my skills are obsolete."

The company's concern:

- The company wants to know if you have the ability to bring your skills up to date and keep them that way. It may also be concerned with why you let your skills get stale and may question your level of motivation and career dedication.

How to overcome this in an interview:

- If you are re-entering the workforce after a significant absence, then your excuse for rusty skills is obvious. If you have taken schooling to update your skills during your absence from the work world, emphasize this. Your schooling will be impressive proof of your dedication and foresight.

Back to School If you have not taken classes to update your skills, it is never too late to begin! Explaining that you are currently enrolled in a class is as impressive as having already taken a class.

- If your skills are rusty for other reasons, emphasize your enthusiasm for bringing them back up to snuff and explain that you are a quick learner. Steer the conversation toward your other skills that are not rusty and use examples that emphasize your self-starter attitude.

SUMMARY

In this lesson you learned the 10 most common interviewing hazards, why interviewers focus on them, and how to handle them effectively in a job interview.

Questions to Answer

In this lesson you learn some of the trickiest questions employers might ask and the secrets behind why they ask them. You also learn the most effective answers for these questions.

Most interviews are structured so that there is a bit of time at the beginning of the meeting to loosen you up a bit. This lead time is meant to ease the pressure, to help you to feel a bit less like an unfamiliar visitor and more like one of the gang. The interviewer sips coffee with you and tells you interesting and pleasant things about the company. But just as you begin to relax, all of a sudden things get tough. Questions that require intelligent answers are thrown at you, and it is time for you to perform.

Whether the interviewer is a friendly sort or not, interview questions are undeniably intimidating. They put you on the spot, demand spur-of-the-moment thinking, and sometimes require artful dodging and creative finesse.

The Interviewer's Task

Turn the interview around in your head for a moment and consider the interviewer's task. He or she has been given the directive to discern not only your strengths for the job the company intends to fill, but also your weaknesses and failure potential.

It is extremely costly to hire employees who do not do the job they were hired to do. There are several possible contributing causes to employee failure. The interviewer's job is to ferret out these potential problems:

- The new hire is not capable of performing the duties of the job (lack of skill or inability to learn new skills).
- The new hire is not able to work with his fellow employees (personality clashes; not a team player).
- The new hire is not able to work with his or her boss (lack of communication; personality clashes; can't follow directions; over-confidence).
- The new hire is not motivated to perform the duties of the job (laziness; bad attitude; distracting private life; position not challenging).
- The new hire plans to leave the company after a short time (will look for a better offer elsewhere).

The interviewer tries to discern, through the questions asked, whether you possess the traits that will make you a happy, healthy, and productive employee.

THE EIGHT KEYS TO ANSWERING INTERVIEW QUESTIONS

Remember eight key points when answering interview questions:

1. **Be Brief.** Each question, no matter how complex, should be answered in 90 seconds or less. Anything beyond that loses the interviewer's interest and

probably involves too much rambling. Be concise, focused, and specific.

2. **Be Positive.** Interviewers try to unearth negatives in your background or personality by asking negative questions. They might ask, "What is your greatest weakness?" "What is the worst failure you've ever had?" or "Tell me about the worst boss you ever had." These questions are designed to get you to spill the beans about things better left unsaid. Remember, you do not need to answer negative questions negatively. Put a positive spin on everything.
3. **State Your Case.** All answers should relate to the heart of the issue: Are you qualified to do the job for which they are hiring? Never lose perspective of this. Look at each question as an opportunity to present your case.
4. **Use Examples.** Don't forget that an integral part of presenting your case is *proving* that you are qualified for the job, not just telling them that you are. This means using examples of past successes to demonstrate your potential for future success.
5. **Identify Results.** Not only must you relate a selection of the wonderful things you have done in the past, but you must also identify the results of those wonderful actions. So what if you devised a new system for tracking incoming customer calls? Was it more efficient than the previous system? Was it less costly? Did it allow for improved customer service? Identify specific ways that your accomplishments and ideas *benefited the company*, and the more specific and quantified your answer is, the better.
6. **Maintain Relevance.** The answers you give to any question should reflect the needs of the company.

It's of no use to you to convince the company that you are a terrific team player if it is hiring you for an independent project that you'll be managing solo. Listen carefully to what is wanted and needed and address those needs specifically in your answers.

7. **Answer Questions with Questions.** A savvy communicator knows that it is not always necessary to answer a question with a direct answer. Sometimes it is better to return the question with a question of your own, especially if you would like to have clearer information before venturing a hasty reply. Asking questions about the questions not only shows that you are intelligent and confident but that you think things through before opening your mouth to speak—a valuable trait in any job.
8. **Break it down.** Interviewers like to see that you can think logically and can break a complex problem down into manageable parts. This works especially well when answering those hypothetical situation questions. Talk about the different areas that need to be addressed and how you would handle them.

SOME BASIC QUESTIONS YOU'LL PROBABLY HEAR

Let's examine some popular interview questions and explore the reasons why they are asked.

TELL ME ABOUT YOURSELF

Why they ask this: On a basic level, this question gives the interviewer an overview of your skills and a logical place to begin. At a deeper level, your answer tells the interviewer how you define yourself by what information you choose to include in your overview. It also allows the interviewer to assess your ability to think on your feet (if, heaven forbid, you are unprepared for such a question) and to create a logical, succinct verbal picture (your communication skills).

How you should answer: This is a great opportunity to present your two-minute bio in all its splendor. (See Lesson 3.) With a well prepared and practiced two-minute bio, you can actually look forward to this question instead of dreading it. And you can bet you're going to get this one; its popularity is on the rise.

Why Should We Hire You?

Why they ask this: The employer wants to hear your interpretation of the important aspects of the job. If you spend your interview for a retail sales position extolling your virtues as a computer expert, you aren't likely to convince the interviewer that you have the skills needed to sell merchandise.

How you should answer: This is another opportunity question: an opportunity to tell how well your skills match the company's needs. If the search is for a super salesperson, tell how well you've honed your skills in persuasion, communication, and perseverance. Give an example of a time that you made a successful sale, or that you convinced someone to do something, or when tenacity paid off.

Bring a Six-Pack Do your homework well. Have at least three strengths and three accomplishments firmly in mind before entering into any interview situation.

Why Do You Want to Work for Our Company?

Why they ask this: In today's world of instant information, you can no longer get away with going into an interview without first having researched the company. The company, in turn, wants to know if you've done your homework.

How you should answer: This question allows you to show off the research you have done on the organization (translate: good work ethic, thorough, detail-oriented, conscientious, enthusiastic, dedicated). Tell the interviewer you like the company's size, location, aggressive market stance, competitive thinking, and creative business policies. It is perfectly acceptable to admit that you looked up the company on the Internet or in the reference section at the library. This shows that you know how to find the answers to questions and arm yourself with information. (See Lesson 4.) This question is popular with interviewers today, so be prepared.

Where Do You See Yourself in Five Years?

Why they ask this: The employer wants to know if you have ambition and realistic, structured goals. The company also wants to know whether you plan to stay for a solid block of time. Occasionally an interviewer unearths some important information regarding a potential employee's longevity by asking this question. If you plan to go to graduate school, take an extended tour of Europe, or move to a distant state, do not mention these plans to the interviewer under any circumstances. You will be considered a hiring risk no matter how strong your skills.

How you should answer: Remember that the main concern throughout the interview is to fill the open position with someone who will be successful in *it*. Say something like,

"First, I'd like to gain a solid foundation in the position you are considering me for, so that I am effective and successful in it. I'm sure that as I continue to grow, there will be opportunities within the company to offer me upward professional growth and new challenges."

Don't Be a Threat Be careful not to sound as if you want to take the boss's job. In today's unstable world of work, you must be careful not to appear threatening.

TELL ME ABOUT A PROBLEM YOU'VE FACED AND HOW YOU HANDLED IT

Why they ask this: They want to assess your analytical skills as well as your ability to relate a delicate situation with tact and diplomacy.

How you should answer: To prevent yourself from stumbling and fumbling for a good response, prepare one before you set foot in the interview. Your answer should involve a clear presentation of the problem, the steps you took to correct the problem, and the results of your actions. Remember to keep it to two minutes, tops.

Don't Degrade Past Co-Workers Do not speak negatively of co-workers or superiors when presenting a scenario. Even if the problem involved gross errors on the part of your fellow employees, do not highlight this. It makes you appear cocky and indiscreet.

WHAT ARE YOUR GREATEST STRENGTHS?

Why they ask this: The interviewer is hoping to hear that your strengths match the needs of the job. He or she also wants to know how you present yourself and will watch warily for overconfidence, boastfulness, dishonesty, and lack of assertiveness.

How you should answer: This is an opportunity to highlight your strong points, so make the most of it. Speak of one or two strengths and then offer examples of how you have used these strengths.

Examples Go a Long Way Tread carefully on that thin line between conceit and modesty. If you can use examples to illustrate why you feel you have certain strengths (or how you have learned them), then you are more likely to impress.

WHAT INTERESTS YOU MOST ABOUT THIS JOB?

Why they ask this: The interviewer is looking for your areas of enthusiasm—where you will put the most energy into the job. Make sure your strong areas match the company's needs.

How you should answer: Answer this question with a question. Ask the interviewer to clarify the position for you before you answer, "so that I can be sure not to miss any key aspects of the job." Then match your interest areas with the key components of the job.

THE TOUGH QUESTIONS

Be prepared for a few zingers that seem as if they were designed to be impossible to answer well. Just remember the seven keys to answering interview questions, and you will find ways to turn such questions into opportunities to shine.

HAVE YOU EVER BEEN FIRED?

Why they ask this: This one's straightforward—to unearth potential problems.

How you should answer: "Fired" generally means that you have been terminated from a job because of performance problems or for other specific causes. If you've never been fired, more power to you. (If you were asked to resign, then you resigned. You were not fired.)

If you have been fired, answer honestly (don't bring it up unless you are asked) and offer a brief, non-accusatory answer. It is best to gently accept the blame yourself, since denouncing a boss or co-workers, no matter how legitimate that may be, only reflects poorly on you. Explain that you have grown from the experience and that you are confident that the difficult times are behind you. Point out successes that you have had since the firing incident.

"Downsized" Does Not Mean "Fired" Do not put yourself in the "fired" category if you have been caught up in a general workforce reduction due to a merger, acquisition, restructuring, and so on. Your job may have been eliminated, but you were not *fired.*

TELL ME ABOUT THE WORST BOSS YOU EVER HAD

Why they ask this: The interviewer wants to know whether you can be tactful and discreet. This is also a way for the company to find out about potential personality clashes that it would rather avoid.

How you should answer: Never shall a negative comment leave your lips. If your bosses were completely insufferable, simply answer with something such as, "I've learned many things from my former bosses: flexibility, perseverance, and the importance of good communication."

Stay Positive Interviewers may ask a variety of these "tell me about the *worst...*" questions. Never let them trick you into saying a negative comment about any former boss, co-worker, position, or company. Always stress the positive behaviors you learned from difficult situations.

RATE YOURSELF ON A SCALE FROM ONE TO TEN

Why they ask this: This question has a high discomfort factor. Aside from enjoying watching you squirm, the interviewer is hoping to see a healthy level of confidence reflected in your answer.

How you should answer: This is one of those questions that is better answered indirectly. You don't have to give a specific number. Telling the interviewer that you see yourself as a ten may be perceived as cocky, as if you feel you have no potential for positive growth. Offering them a seven, eight, or nine, however, may give the appearance that you are under-confident or are not a high achiever.

The safest answer is something like, "I'm always striving for a ten in all aspects of my life, professional as well as personal. It's important to me to be the best that I can be in all the things I strive to do."

WHAT ARE YOUR GREATEST WEAKNESSES?

Why they ask this: It is unlikely that most interviewers are straining their ears to hear your list of weaknesses. They simply want to see how well you handle the question.

How you should answer: Some job candidates can get away with an answer like, "While I certainly have weaknesses, I don't believe I have any that are significant to the success of this position. As you've described the position to me, I think it would allow me to call upon my strengths."

If you don't feel you could pull that off, name a weakness that is first, not closely related to the position for which you are interviewing, and second, a technical skill that you can easily learn rather than a shortcoming in your personality, which is very difficult to change. Then tell the interviewer how you are working to improve your weak spot. An example: "I've gotten a bit rusty in my hands-on production skills since becoming a manager. Now I spend my time finding solutions to production problems from the broader perspective, but I try to get in with the workers and do hands-on work now and then so that I can understand the workers' needs and stay on top of production changes."

Practice on Your Friends Try a few answers to these difficult questions on your friends. Ask for honest feedback about the broader connotations of your answers from an interviewer's perspective.

ARE YOU A LEADER OR FOLLOWER?

Why they ask this: The interviewer is digging into personality dynamics here. This is the most dangerous of issues for you.

How you should answer: Most job candidates assume that the winning side to this coin is the "leader" answer. Certainly, having leadership ability is a positive trait. But what if the interviewer is concerned about a potential employee's ability to follow directions well? A safe and strong answer is this: "In my many years of experience, I've learned to be both a leader and a follower. I've learned the importance of listening well and being an integral part of a team effort. I've also had the opportunity to lead on several projects and have found that I am effective and successful as a leader." Feel free to throw in a specific example of an accomplishment here.

SUMMARY

In this lesson, you learned the seven secrets to answering interview questions. You reviewed sample interview questions and guidelines for successful answers.

Using Examples

In this lesson you learn how to impress the interviewer by proving your skills and abilities through the use of examples of past performance.

For those of us who are on the shy and quiet side, interviews can be very frustrating experiences. We need to tell the interviewer how good we are and how hard we work, yet we just can't seem to make any of the words come out of our mouths in a convincing fashion. We want to make the interviewer believe in our ability, yet we don't have the skills and panache to be convincing and persuasive.

There is, however, one foolproof way to convince a potential employer of your skills and qualities. It does not involve undue amounts of charisma nor elocution skills. It involves only one artifice: the use of examples.

Prove It

How do you convince a potential employer that you have the skills and traits she is looking for? The secret to an impressive interview is the ability to *prove your strengths and skills through examples of past performance.*

Results Are the Key Employers know that the best predictor of how well you will do on a new job is not what you did on a past job but *how well you did it.*

Anyone can say the words, "I am a leader," or "I am creative," but only the people who really are those things can provide examples from their experience to back these words. The interviewer draws conclusions about how successfully you can use your skills to achieve results for him on the basis of your past accomplishments and experiences.

Use Examples from Anywhere Examples of achievements outside of the workplace can be just as effective as examples of professional achievements.

PROVE THE RIGHT THING

It is of no use to spend the entire interview convincing a potential employer that you are full of creativity when creativity is not important to him. Spend your time with the interviewer wisely by emphasizing the skills you have that *relate to the job at hand.*

Before answering any questions, such as "Tell me about yourself," or "Why do you think you are right for this job?" ask the interviewer to tell you a bit about the position she is trying to fill. This is certainly a legitimate question on your part, asked so that you have a better understanding of the position before you begin answering questions. You can explain to the interviewer, if you feel you should, that having a description of the position will allow you to answer her questions in a more targeted fashion. This way, you can get a feel for the skills that will be most useful for performing the job successfully, and you can spend your time emphasizing those.

EXERCISE 1: ANSWERING QUESTIONS WITH EXAMPLES OF EXPERIENCE

Try answering the following questions using examples from your own experience.

Read the sample answers for ideas.

"WHAT ARE YOUR GREATEST STRENGTHS?"

Poor Answer: *Well, I feel I'm very tenacious. I can stick to a project even when the going gets tough.*

Comments: In the answer above, the job candidate used the right kind of words in her answer: Tenacity is a personality trait that any potential employer eagerly listens for. Her mistake was in the way she presented her case, or lack thereof. What she told the interviewer was not in the least bit convincing. You must realize that most interviewers expect to hear pretty words. But they won't believe them unless you prove your case with examples.

Great Answer: *One personal trait I've found very useful in my years as a sales manager is my tenacity. In one case in particular, this paid off very well. I had been trying to get my foot in the door with A.P. Robs Company and had been finding them very inaccessible. After countless phone calls and fruitless visits, I continued to pursue them. Finally, I ran into a key player for Robs at an association meeting. I sat next to him at the luncheon and managed to weave in some business talk along with the casual. In the following* *weeks, I landed a contract with Robs worth $16 million to the company.*

Comments: In her second answer, the job candidate does prove her case. She introduces the word *tenacity* as one of the skills she ranks as a greatest strength, and then goes on to explain how she has used this skill to achieve results. In this case, the interviewer can draw his own conclusions about the job applicant from the information he's been given through her use of examples. From this particular story, the interviewer sees a potential employee who is motivated, tenacious, clever, determined, confident, and a good persuader.

"WHY SHOULD WE HIRE YOU?"

Poor Answer: *I'm dedicated, and I can work hard even through tough situations.*

Comments: Again, nice words in the first answer, but no persuasive proof to back the words up.

Great Answer: *You'll find that I am a dedicated worker even when the going gets tough. In this most recent year at school, for example, I had a heavy class load of 21 credit hours plus a 30-hour per week job to help me pay for school. During this time I chaired a committee to redesign a student quad on the central campus and earned additional credits as a student assistant in the business school. All the while, I kept my focus on my studies and maintained a 3.5 grade point average.*

Comments: The job candidate's second answer is much more effective and convincing than the first because the example she uses helps the interviewer to arrive at her own positive conclusions about the applicant. The interviewer can see that the candidate is hardworking, motivated, a leader, resourceful, and intelligent.

Practice Your Stories Practice and preparation are very important to a polished presentation. If you must continually backtrack, revise, or reword your illustration, it will not only be unimpressive but will be irritating as well.

EXERCISE 2: MATCHING YOUR EXPERIENCES TO SKILLS

Try to come up with stories from your own experience that demonstrate, through example, the fact that you possess the following personality traits or skills. It is better to relate clear, interesting illustrations from your professional experience, but stories from your personal background can be just as effective. You may be able to refer to the exercise you completed in Lesson 2, "Evaluating Skills."

Answer in Under a Minute Keep the answers to a reasonable length: about 30 to 60 seconds of speaking time. Wordiness only dilutes the message and diffuses the power of your story.

1. **Hardworking:** Was there a time in your career that you were challenged by a particularly difficult project that required extra energy to complete? Describe it.

2. **Persuasive:** Have you ever had to overcome resistance and convince someone that a project should be completed differently or a problem should be handled in a different way? Describe it.

3. **Self-motivated:** Have you ever taken on a project on your own initiative or gone beyond the call of duty in a certain situation? Describe it.
4. **Leadership:** Have you coordinated a program or managed a group of people on a project? Describe it.
5. **Creativity:** Are you the type who likes to design or invent? Have you ever visualized creative ways to improve efficiency? Describe a time that your creativity lead to a new or improved product.

Don't Recycle Stories Never tell the same story to illustrate two different skills. It is much more impressive to have several stories to use as examples of your talents and skills.

Explain Without Bragging Be careful to relate your examples to the interviewer in a way that is not boastful or arrogant. Never belittle co-workers, scoff at your current or former company, or speak badly of anyone. This only makes you look petty and egotistical. Present your achievements in a way that emphasizes your appreciation of others and a satisfaction in being able to put your skills to use to make a positive change for the company.

SUMMARY

In this lesson you learned the importance of proving your case through the use of examples and practiced developing tactics for a powerful, convincing interview performance.

Questions to Ask

In this lesson you learn how to ask questions that emphasize your strengths and bring the interview to a strong and positive conclusion.

Interviewers ask many tough questions throughout the course of an interview, and coming up with convincing, sincere answers is vital to the success of the meeting. But few people realize that one of the trickiest questions that an interviewer may ask a job applicant is, "Do you have any questions you would like to ask of us?"

The questions you choose to ask are an opportunity for the interviewer to assess your understanding of the position, your knowledge of the industry, your business savvy, and your motivation for wanting the job. It can also reveal concerns and fears you may have about the position and other negatives that are better left unsaid. How do you know what questions to ask? Use these guidelines:

Tips for Asking Questions

- Have a list of prepared questions handy when you go in to the interview. It is perfectly fine to refer to them openly; this shows the interviewer preparedness and organization skills as well as enthusiasm for the job.

- You may take notes throughout the interview (it might be polite to ask if you may) and then refer to them during question time.

The Goal of Asking Questions The questions you ask should focus on gaining more information about the job and company so that you can make an informed decision about how you can help them. You don't want to focus your questions on how the company can help you or what your expectations are of it. There will be time for these questions *when you get the offer.*

- Make the interviewer think of you as an employee of the company by writing yourself into the script whenever possible. For example, ask "What are the projects that *I* would be devoting the most attention to?" instead of "What are the projects that *the person you hire* would be devoting the most attention to?"
- Never ask a question or make a comment that reveals former problems or failures, such as, "You said we won't be doing any computer work, right? Because I tried working on a computer once, and I just couldn't figure it out." This shows a lack of willingness to learn or to accept new challenges.

Don't Mention Anything Negative Remember that the interviewer is trying to unearth your potential negatives as well as your positives. Don't give her anything to be concerned about, no matter how insignificant it may seem to you. These are the little slips that lose job offers.

- Don't ask questions that reveal lack of enthusiasm for the job, such as, "Will you be asking us to work a lot of overtime?" or "Are those reports you mentioned we'd be writing really *long?*" These statements are interpreted as negative statements: "I don't want to work overtime, and I don't like working hard."
- Don't create negative scenarios: "What happens if I show up late more than three times?" or "What should I do if I have to call in sick?" These questions raise red flags for the interviewer.

QUESTIONS THAT SELL

One of the best things about your opportunity to ask questions of the interviewer is that it buys you a chance to end the interview on a positive note by reiterating one last time the positive things about yourself in relation to the job. Seize this opportunity and give it all you've got.

SELLER QUESTION GUIDELINES

- Make sure you have been paying attention throughout the job interview so that you can use this time to *match* your skills with the skills that are crucial to this particular job. You should have asked early on in the interview, "What projects will I be involved with in the first few months?" or "What are the most important aspects of the position you are trying to fill?" If you haven't asked those questions yet, ask them now! If you haven't had a chance to talk up those skills enough during the interview, do it now!
- Ask questions that reveal your research of the company: "I noticed in your annual report that your firm

has made several acquisitions lately. Is this aggressive business stance likely to continue?"

- Ask questions in a way that gives you a chance to show off a bit: "You mentioned as part of the job description that I would be designing new market strategies for your new line of hair-care products. At XYZ Company, I was doing something very similar with a line of skin-care products. Our timelines there were often very short, and we had to keep up the hustle to get the products launched on time. I managed a team of eight, and I'm proud to say we never missed a deadline. Can you tell me about the timelines that I'd be facing here?"
- Ask questions that reveal your understanding of the key aspects and challenges of the position: "You mentioned that it can sometimes be difficult to motivate the technicians when a new line is being introduced. I faced this same problem as a manager at XYZ. Last year I introduced some creative scheduling ideas that the technicians responded to well. My ideas alleviated the rushed feeling technicians had during the quick turnaround time between projects at XYZ. What kind of turnaround time do you have here at your company?"

Don't Try to Save the World Be wary of proposing solutions to cure company problems right there in the interview. While you may feel that you have a great idea to present, the interviewer could perceive you as arrogant or unrealistic if you propose solutions to problems about which you have little knowledge.

- Let the interviewer do a little talking. Ask why she joined the company, how long she's been there, and what she likes best about the company. She may let down her guard a bit and give you some solid information.

Ask to See the Boss A wise move is to ask if you might have a chance to meet your potential future boss during the interview process. This allows you to assess your chemistry together and gives you a chance to impress another key person in the hiring decision.

QUESTIONS THAT BUY

Your time to ask questions is not only a chance to market yourself to the employer one last time, it also allows you to ask some important questions to help you assess the company for which you may some day be working. This is the right time for you to find out information about the company and the position that it is attempting to fill. But be careful: Some questions have a certain time sensitivity of which you must be aware.

BUYER QUESTION GUIDELINES

- Under no circumstances should you ask questions in regard to salary, benefits, or other compensation until a specific job offer has been made.
- You might be smart to ask why the position is open. Some interviewers incautiously may let some very interesting cats out of the bag in their responses.

What Are You Getting Into? Ask why the last person to hold the job left. Was he promoted within the company? Was he fired? Has this position experienced heavy turnover? These questions give you insight into the expectations for the position.

- To gain particularly clear insight into potential problems and unspoken expectations, ask how well the job has been performed in the past. You may unearth vital and surprising information about messy situations that you'll be expected to fix.
- It is perfectly appropriate to ask the interviewer how your performance would be measured on the job. This helps you discern expectations and the organizational structure.
- Clarify what resources you will have available to accomplish your objectives. The more solid the figures on staff and budget, the better.
- Ask the name and job title of the person to whom you would report. Ask how long that person has been there and how many people report to him or her.

THE THREE KEY ASPECTS OF THE JOB

The questions you ask should be used to assess three aspects of the potential job offer. These questions may be asked at any point during the interview:

1. The Job

(What will they expect of you?)

- What are the responsibilities of this position?
- What is the first challenge that needs attention?
- What are the key strengths you are looking for in the person you hire?

2. Colleagues and Associates

(Will you have supportive and knowledgeable colleagues?)

- You said I would be reporting to Mr. Smith. Can you tell me about his management style?
- Do you have plans to reduce or increase staff levels?
- How is the morale in the division in which I would work?

3. The Organization

(Is the company firmly rooted and growing?)

- How does your company stand apart from its competition?
- Is the company in a growth phase?
- How do you see the future of this industry?
- Does the company have a mission or vision statement?
- How is your company reaching for that vision today?

Summary

In this lesson you learned how to ask questions that will impress the interviewer and allow you to collect vital information about your potential new job.

LESSON 15

Illegal Questions

In this lesson you learn the questions that are illegal and that should not be a part of the job interview. You also learn the appropriate way to handle such questions if they are asked.

Legal Guidelines

Employers are bound by a set of legal guidelines to avoid certain questions during a selection interview. The following guidelines give an overview of the questions that interviewers legally can or cannot ask.

Race or Color

Can't Ask: No questions may be asked about your race or color.

Religion or Creed

Can't Ask: Questions may not be asked about your religious denomination, affiliations, church, synagogue, parish, pastor, rabbi, or religious holidays observed.

Can Ask: If you will be consistently required to work on a day that is a sabbath for a religion, the interviewer may ask if the work schedule will cause conflict with religious values.

NATIONAL ORIGIN

Can't Ask: You may not be asked about your ancestry, national origin, descent, parentage, nationality, or your spouse's lineage.

MARITAL STATUS

Can't Ask: An interviewer may not ask questions about marital status, children, children's ages, or where your spouse is employed.

GENDER

Can't Ask: No questions may be asked regarding your gender, nor about your sexual orientation.

AGE

Can Ask: The interviewer may ask you if you are between the ages of eighteen and seventy. If you say that you are not, the interviewer may ask when you were born or what your exact age is.

HANDICAP STATUS

Can Ask: The interviewer may ask if you have any impairments, physical or mental, that could interfere with the ability to perform the job. You may be asked if there are any positions for which you should not be considered because of a physical or mental handicap.

Can't Ask: The interviewer may not, however, ask if you are handicapped, if you have been treated for any diseases, or if a member of your family has had any disease.

NAME

Can Ask: You may be asked if you have ever worked for the organization under a different name or if you use a nickname or an assumed name.

Can't Ask: An interviewer may not ask your maiden name. You cannot be asked if your name has ever been changed by court action or if you have ever worked under another name.

ADDRESS

Can Ask: The interviewer may ask your place of residence and how long you have been a resident of the city or state.

Can't Ask: The interviewer may not ask if you own or rent your residence.

BIRTHPLACE

Can't Ask: Interviewers may not ask you where you, your parents, spouse, children, or other close relatives were born.

CITIZENSHIP

Can Ask: You may be asked if you are a citizen of the United States. If not, you may be asked about your intention to become a citizen and if you can legally remain in the U.S. You may be asked if you were ever arrested as a non-citizen.

Can't Ask: Interviewers may not ask your specific country of citizenship or whether you or your spouse or parents are native born or naturalized.

LANGUAGE

Can Ask: You may be asked what languages you are able to speak, read, or write.

EDUCATION

Can Ask: The interviewer may ask about your education and training, including types of courses studied, courses completed, and grades achieved.

EXPERIENCE

Can Ask: Interviewers may ask about all aspects of your job-related work experience.

CHARACTER

Can Ask: You may be asked if you have ever been convicted of a crime and if so, when, where, and disposition of the offense.

Can't Ask: The interviewer may not ask if you have ever been arrested.

RELATIVES

Can Ask: The interviewer may ask the names of any relatives who are already employed by the organization.

Can't Ask: The interviewer may not ask about any relatives not employed by the organization.

Military Experience

Can Ask: The interviewer may ask if you have been a member of the armed forces and about any training or experience you have had in the armed forces that relates to the position for which you are applying. You may be asked whether you were discharged and when.

Can't Ask: You may not be asked what type of discharge you received from the armed forces.

Organizations

Can Ask: You may be asked if you belong to any club or organization.

Can't Ask: You may not be asked to list or identify all the clubs or organizations to which you belong.

References

Can Ask: The interviewer may ask you to supply names of references and to specify how you came to apply for the position.

How to Respond to Illegal Questions

It is really quite unlikely that you will run into a blatantly illegal question. Many employers are well aware of the implications of asking illegal questions in the interview and carefully steer clear of them.

If you do find yourself in the uncomfortable position of having to answer an illegal question, use the following guidelines:

1. Be brief
2. Be positive

While you may be tempted to argue the value of the question, it is better to control your anger and avoid getting defensive. This will only be seen as confrontational and will not improve your chances of getting hired. Answer the question quickly, and give it a positive spin. For example:

"How many children do you have?"

Their fears: Your children will distract you from your work.

Your answer: "I have two, and I'm quite proud of them. They are proud of me, too, and of my accomplishments in my career. They understand how important my work is to me, and they do not interfere with my career life."

"How old are you?"

Their fears: You are too young to have a thorough understanding of the job; or, you are tired and ready to retire after a couple years of earning a paycheck.

Your answer: Be vague. Cleverly avoid an exact age by using a rounded number, such as "I'm in my mid 40s." Or, you might try, "Old enough to have built an extensive base of industry knowledge, and I am looking forward to continuing to grow in the field for many more years."

SUMMARY

In this lesson you learned the legal guidelines that interviewers follow when asking interview questions and how to deal with illegal questions if they should be asked.

LESSON 16

The Thank-You Note

In this lesson you learn the proper techniques for writing interview thank-you notes and the best strategies to communicate your strengths through the thank-you letter.

Thank-you letters are not to be overlooked; they are an important and effective part of your interview presentation. The thank-you letter tells the potential employer that you are enthusiastic about the prospect of working for the organization and demonstrates your follow-through, initiative, and professional courtesy.

When to Write a Thank-You Note

A thank-you letter must be written after each formal job interview, regardless of whether the interview is long or short, conducted in person or over the telephone (except for quick HR screening interviews), or whether it is likely to result in a job offer. The letter should be sent no later than two to three business days after the interview is completed.

Do not wait. There are no legitimate reasons to postpone the sending of a thank-you letter, even if you think you will be made a job offer before the company could possibly receive it.

A well-written thank-you note can only work in your favor and can do you no harm. Of course, a thank-you note must never be poorly written nor contain grammatical and spelling errors.

Think Long-Term Send a thank-you letter even if you are not interested in the job or the company you interviewed for. You never know who that person may know or for what other positions your résumé might be forwarded.

WHO SHOULD BE SENT A THANK-YOU LETTER?

The thank-you letter should be sent to everyone who was formally involved in the interview process. This includes not only the primary interviewer (the person who initiated the interview) but also any other people who may have sat in on a portion of the interview or with whom you engaged in significant discussion. A thank-you note does not need to be sent to the receptionist, secretaries, or people whom you met only briefly, unless the interaction was outstanding in some way and warrants special attention.

Be careful to spell all names correctly, and to use proper job titles. Calling someone a product manager when his or her actual title is Product Management Director can be a costly mistake.

Be sure not to send an exact duplicate to each person. Each letter should be unique and should address the unique interaction you had with that individual.

Get the Names Right Never guess on the spelling of the interviewer's name or job title on the thank-you note. Even the name "Smith" has several possible spellings! If you are unsure of the spelling when you are ready to write the letter, call the office and ask the receptionist for name spelling and formal job title.

THE PROPER STYLE FOR A THANK-YOU LETTER

A thank-you letter should remain professional in style, although it does not have to be cold or impersonal. It should be written on fine-quality white or cream bond paper of standard size, 8 1/2 × 11". A matching, professional-size envelope looks nice, with a typed address and return address. Do not hand write your letter. A typewritten letter makes a much more professional presentation.

Casual Words, Formal Paper Do not use note cards or flowery stationery, no matter how informal the interview. Make the tone of the letter casual by using casual words rather than by using casual paper.

The letter should be kept short. Do not extend beyond one page. A concise letter is much more enjoyable to read than a sprawling epic.

WHAT TO INCLUDE IN YOUR THANK-YOU LETTER

The thank-you letter is more than a simple "thank-you for your time" note. Use the letter to highlight your interest and strengths and to renew the personal contact.

THE OPENING

A good thank-you note opens with the reason for sending the letter. It gets right to the point:

> "Dear Mr. Smith: I am sending you this note to thank you for the intriguing meeting we had on Wednesday."

Or:

> "Dear Jim: I enjoyed meeting you on Monday to discuss the operations management position. Your description of the position piqued my interest, especially in the direct services area."

THE BODY OF THE LETTER

The body of the thank-you note can contain several important sections:

- **The Personal Touch:** Each thank-you note should be uniquely written to mention specific aspects of the interview.

  For example: "You mentioned that the Product Division will be launching a new line early next year."

  Or: "You mentioned that an important aspect of the position would be keeping firm control of incoming product orders, as you have just updated to a new, unfamiliar computerized tracking system."

Add a Personal Touch To set a friendly and more casual tone, you may also mention some of the more personal things you may have discussed in the interview: a favorite author, a mutual acquaintance, an upcoming vacation, and sc on.

Referring to specific statements that the interviewer made and keying in on the things that the interviewer considers important aspects of the position shows that you were paying attention in the interview and that you are savvy enough to recognize the needs of the organization.

- **The Skills Reinforcement:** Once you have mentioned the key aspects of your potential new position, reinforce your strengths by emphasizing how your strengths fit the company's needs.

  For example: "In my 12 years at XYZ Inc., I oversaw the launching of five successful new product lines and became familiar with all aspects of a new product campaign."

  Or: "While at Dresner, I managed the transition from an outdated, manual tracking system to an automated, computerized system that was used by over 15 customer service professionals. I initiated training programs that reduced error rate and established policies to ensure quick and accurate product turnaround."

  This section expresses an understanding of the organization's needs and confidence in your ability to fill those needs.

- **Enthusiasm for the Position:** It is important to state your interest in the position, if you do indeed have any. Make your letter stand out because of your excitement over the possibilities.

Remember to Say You Want the Job Don't assume that the company knows you want the job simply because you have written a letter. State it outright, such as, "I am enthusiastic about the prospect of joining your company" or "I am eager for the opportunity to bring my expertise in marketing to your organization."

- **Clear-up of Misconceptions:** If you felt that there may have been some misunderstanding that occurred during the interview—perhaps you answered a question in a way that you later thought was presenting your skills in an unflattering light—now is the time to right the wrong.

Don't Make It Harder for Yourself Do not call undue attention to small matters. You don't want to make mountains out of what may have been mere molehills to the interviewer.

For example: "Because of the challenges involved in the position as you described it, I'd like to reiterate my strengths to emphasize my ability to meet those challenges." Then reword the answer to the question you flubbed to put your skills in a more positive light, one that reflects the needs of the company.

- **The "I should have saids...":** The body of the thank-you note is a good place to bring up any information that you may have forgotten to bring up in the interview. This gives you a chance to answer that nagging feeling that you left out vital information, the absence of which may cost you the job. Again, the new information should be added in terms so as to address company needs, when possible.

  For example: "As you mentioned your company's important new international connections, I was reminded of my role as manufacturing coordinator with ABC Corp. There I dealt with manufacturers in 11 non-English-speaking countries where customs and traditions are very different from those in the U.S. I found the position both challenging and enlightening, and I feel I could draw on my background with international manufacturing to make a smooth transition into your company as international liaison for operations."

THE CLOSE

The closing paragraph of the thank-you note should include a mention of your interest in the position, if you haven't already done this. It should also explicitly refer to the next steps in the process. For example,

> "I'll look forward to your call on Friday afternoon, as you mentioned during the interview."

Or, if no further action was indicated in the interview, you might say, "I will call you late next week to touch base if I have not heard from you by that time."

This is also a good place to make reference to lighter topics that emerged in the interview, such as,

"Meanwhile, I'll keep you posted on that annual conference we discussed. If I should receive any information on it, I'll send it along."

FOLLOWING UP

It is perfectly fine to follow up by telephone with the interviewer after a certain amount of time has passed, especially if it is past the agreed-upon date that you expected to hear from him or her. Use this opportunity to express your continued interest in the position, but do not jeopardize your chances by taking up the person's time with extended questions on the status of the position.

Spend the Call Wisely Concentrate your follow-up call on the person who has the power to hire, rather than the human resources department. Try to talk directly with the hiring manager who interviewed you.

Don't Write Yourself into a Corner If you say in your thank-you note that you will follow up with a telephone call at a later date, you must remain true to your word. Don't pin yourself down to a specific date and time for the follow-up call. Give yourself a time frame of several days, such as "I will follow up with you later in the week," or "by early next week."

EXAMPLES

(date)

Joel Perryson
Director, Marketing Division
Blee Company
7266 Wyehill Rd.
Thompsonville, CA 90341

Dear Joel:

I enjoyed meeting with you yesterday to discuss the marketing manager position you have available in the Brokerton office.

In our meeting, you discussed the importance of a new vision for the regional offices and a possible restructuring of the field organization. While at Memix, I successfully restructured our field divisions from 12 to 9 regions while increasing the capabilities of our service delivery.

You also mentioned the importance of maintaining strong customer relationships. I agree that the ability to maintain and enhance customer connections is a vital part of any marketing program. While at Memix, I have written and facilitated several workshops to train our marketing professionals in building customer relationships. And while I am no longer in the field, I maintain close associations with the top management level of over 10 major accounts.

I was very enthusiastic about Blee's vision and direction, and I was very impressed with the friendly, professional atmosphere at Blee.

I look forward to hearing from you in regard to the management position. If I have not heard from you by the middle of the month, I will call to check on the progress of your decision. In the meantime, enjoy your trip to beautiful Hawaii!

Sincerely,

Jaime Flouers

(date)

Ms. Taylor Schuren
Vice President, Financial Services
H.R. Daniels and Sons
165 West 4th Street
Morristown, NJ 07201

Dear Ms. Schuren:

Thank you for meeting with me on Thursday. I enjoyed learning about the administrative assistant position you have available in the Financial Services office.

In our meeting you highlighted the need for an administrative assistant who can work independently to ensure a smooth work flow in your busy office. My three years of experience assisting in the administrative operations of a 12-person high-volume procurement office has taught me to organize and prioritize my work assignments so that I can accomplish them independently and efficiently.

You also emphasized a need for a responsive and cheerful attitude in dealing with your many clients. I have had much direct client contact in several of my past positions, and I find dealing with customers to be one of the most rewarding and energizing aspects of my career.

I believe that I can be a valuable member of your office team and am enthusiastic about the prospect of working in the team-oriented, goal-directed atmosphere I observed while visiting with you.

I look forward to hearing from you soon. I will follow up with you late next week if I have not heard from you by then.

Sincerely,
Kiera Chase

SUMMARY

In this lesson, you learned how to write a thank-you letter that will work to your advantage in being offered the position.

LESSON 17

SALARY NEGOTIATION

In this lesson you learn how to ensure the highest possible salary for yourself when you accept a new job.

Negotiating a salary and benefits package is one of the most difficult, yet potentially most rewarding, aspects of the job search. Talking turkey always makes us a bit uncomfortable, for many possible reasons:

- Perhaps we feel a bit greedy asking for more money from the people who obviously like us and are nice enough to offer us a job.
- Deep down inside we may be a bit uneasy about whether we actually deserve the bigger bucks we're asking for.
- We are afraid that if we appear too greedy the job offer may be withdrawn.
- Most of us don't have a lot of practice in negotiating skills, and we're afraid we're completely out of our league.
- Maybe we're worried that if we don't negotiate well enough we could end up with much less than we might have had.

How can you lessen your anxiety over the negotiation process and increase your prospects of coming out ahead at the same time? Just a little preparation goes a long way toward making the most of a negotiating opportunity. Once you are familiar with the rules of the game, it's easy to develop a winning strategy.

THE SEVEN RULES TO REMEMBER WHEN NEGOTIATING SALARY

A few basic principles to salary negotiation are important to follow carefully:

1. KNOW YOUR BOTTOM LINE

Whether you are negotiating for a new car, a new house, or a new job, it is always important to know your bottom line going into the deal. Do this in three steps:

Step 1.

- Hone in on the figure that fits in the blank, "I absolutely cannot accept a position that pays less than $______."
- Be realistic. If this were an absolutely wonderful company with wonderful growth potential and other good perks, what would be the absolute lowest salary you would accept? If this is a marginal company of lesser interest to you, what would be the lowest salary you would accept?

Once you have determined this figure for each individual company with which you interview, store it in your head and keep it hidden there. This figure is for no ears to hear. It is simply a guidepost for you at one end of your negotiation parameters.

Step 2.

- Now identify a second figure. This is a realistic salary expectation based upon your value in the current market. Ask headhunters for advice on where you fit into the market monetarily or speak to others in the field who hold similar positions. You might also check the library for reference books on the subject. Find out where you fit in and fill in the blank to the statement, "I would be happy with a salary offer of $________."

This will be your middle point.

Step 3.

- The third figure you should identify before entering into negotiations is the salary that would raise your eyebrows at the very mention of it: the salary you never really thought you could possibly get. Arrive at this figure by adding 20% to 30% to the annual figure in Step 2. Fill in the blank to this sentence: "I would be extremely happy with an offer of $__________."

You have now identified a starting point, a mid-point, and a high point to your salary possibilities.

2. Let the Company Start the Money Talk First

It is wise to let the company open the door to the salary issue. In all cases, do not bring up the subject of salary until the deal has progressed quite far and the possibility of an offer is strong. In fact, if you suspect that the salary will be somewhere in the right ballpark anyway, it is safer to put off salary talks until an offer is made.

You may be tempted to argue that this seems foolish, since the salary you are offered will play a very significant part in your decision whether or not to work there, and it could be a waste of everyone's time to continue with a series of interviews if the company can't come up with an appropriate salary for you.

But talking money too soon can only do you harm. If you insist upon a high salary early in the game, you may knock yourself right out of the running. Once the company has made the commitment to hire you, it will be more willing to increase the salary to meet your needs.

Don't Focus on Money Until Later An early interview is simply too soon to be getting down to financial details. Wait until you have convinced them that you are the best person for the job and they have chosen you as the person they want to hire before you begin to discuss salary.

3. Avoid Money Talk, Even if the Interviewer Brings Up the Subject

Occasionally, an employer throws out a money question in the very first interview. She may ask something like, "What would it take to make you happy here?" or "What are your salary expectations for this position?" The best answer for such questions is, "I'm quite flexible in terms of salary," or "I am looking for a salary that is suitable for my experience and skills as they relate to the challenges of this position." Naming a figure at this point is a mistake.

4. He Who Speaks First Loses

The subject of salary can arise at many places and times long before an interview has reached the serious stage.

- Newspaper employment ads often ask you to submit "salary history" or "salary expectations" along with your résumé.

  Respond to this request with a polite statement, "My salary expectations are open." or "My salary history has been progressively competitive," and leave it at that. Only if the ad states that you *must submit salary information in order to be considered for the position,* should you oblige with the requested figure.

- In a screening interview, the human resources department may ask you to name a figure, either your current salary or your salary expectations.

  Respond to this with polite vagueness. "My current salary is competitive in the market" or "I am open in terms of salary." Or, you might try, "It would be helpful to learn some background on the position first before we discuss salary."

- When filling out a job application, you often run across a spot to list past salaries.

  Application blocks typically ask for a salary background. When filling in these blocks, remember that offering this information up front can only hurt you in the negotiation process. For salary requirements, list "open" or "negotiable." When the application form asks for salary history, say "progressively competitive."

5. ALWAYS SPEAK IN TERMS OF RANGES

When you are asked to give your salary requirements, whether it is on the application, in the screening interview, or even in answering the employment ad, giving a solid figure can be deadly.

Let's say you tell them you are looking for $40,000. What if they were hoping to offer only $35,000? You may have knocked yourself out of the game before you had a chance to convince them that you were worth the extra $5,000. On the other hand, if you tell them you would like $40,000, and they had been willing to pay $50,000, how do you think this will affect the offer? Will they still offer you $50,000? Doubtful.

Be as vague as possible when answering questions about salary history or salary expectations. And if you get backed into a corner on it, offer a range. "My most recent salary was in the $40,000 to $50,000 range," or "My salary expectations are in the $40,000 to $50,000 range."

Don't Narrow it Down Remember that all jobs have salary ranges attached to them. If you mention your salary expectations in terms of ranges rather than one solid figure, you are increasing your chances of getting a higher salary at offer time.

6. SPEAK OF YOUR MARKET VALUE, NOT OF YOUR NEEDS

So what if you have a big mortgage, a new baby, a big car payment, and college tuition to manage into your budget? The employer may be sympathetic, but these expenses will not convince her to pay you a higher salary.

An employer can justify paying you more money only if you convince her that you are worth the money to her, that you offer unique and valuable skills that are worth the extra dollars.

The easiest way to convince an employer of your worth is to relate your skills and qualifications in terms of his needs for the position.

Focus on the Challenging Aspects of the Job Always present the position in terms of its most challenging aspects and how you can meet those challenges. Belittling the job as you speak of it could lessen the salary the company decides to offer.

Justify Your Request Give the employer good reasons to give you the higher salary figure you request. Justify it with solid examples of past performance, accomplishments, and successes so that your interviewer can champion your case with upper management.

7. Understand the Bounds of Reality

While we would all like to make a high six-figure salary, most of us don't. And while we absolutely must shoot for the highest reasonable salary when negotiating an offer, we must understand what is realistic. Some basic guidelines:

- The higher the position level, the easier it is to negotiate. Entry-level positions tend to have little negotiating room. On the other hand, negotiations are expected for lower-, middle-, and upper-level management positions.

- Negotiating a 10- to 20-percent increase over the salary originally offered to you is not unreasonable.
- Begin by asking for a 20- to 25-percent increase over the potential employer's first offer. Remember, it is always easier to negotiate down than it is to negotiate up.
- Never begin negotiations by mentioning your current salary. Your future salary should be based upon your value in the market and your value to the potential employer, not on your salary history.

HOW TO PLAY THE RANGE GAME AT OFFER TIME

It is important to remember this rule, even at offer time:

He who speaks first loses.

If you can enter the negotiations armed with knowledge about what the employer is willing to pay, without having revealed what you are willing to take, you are in the best possible negotiating position.

Let's look at an example:

The interviewer turns to you and says, "We like your qualifications and would like to bring you on board. How much will it take to get you?"

You answer wisely by saying, "I'm hoping for a salary that matches my skills and experience. What is the salary range for this position?"

The interviewer answers that the salary range is between $40,000 and $45,000.

Good! You have managed to get the interviewer to reveal the salary range to you before you have revealed any figures yourself. Armed with this information, you can now adjust your salary range to encompass what the company has to offer. Remember, don't shoot for the lower end of the range even if that is what you had originally intended.

Use this knowledge to give yourself a possible salary boost:

> "That range sounds similar to what I had in mind. I am looking for no less than $42,000 with an ideal of $47,000."

Now ask a vital question, and be sure to word it just this way:

> "Do you have any flexibility at the top of your salary range?"

While you may not get them to blow the roof out of the top of their range, you are at least encouraging them to think at the upper end of the range.

Employers Start on the Low End Employers usually have a salary range in mind for each position, and their first offer will typically be at the lower end of that range to allow room for negotiating.

Negotiating Is Like Gravity It is always easier to negotiate down than it is to negotiate up. Start with an amount that is at the top end of your range so that you are still satisfied if you must move downward a bit.

SUMMARY

In this lesson you learned effective negotiating strategies to ensure a satisfactory salary at the start of a new job.

LESSON 18

Benefits Packages

In this lesson you learn what to look for in benefits options and receive suggestions on how to negotiate aspects of the job offer other than salary.

Negotiating Beyond Salary

It is easier to negotiate your annual salary figure than it is to negotiate any other part of your compensation package. Employers simply have more flexibility on salaries (because they typically have a set salary range for the position within which they can move) than they do for other parts of the compensation package.

In some cases, however, the salary simply cannot be brought up to the goals and expectations that you had at the start of the negotiation process. If the salary offer falls a bit short of satisfactory, you may want to try stating,

"While I'm enthusiastic about the prospect of joining your company, frankly I'm a little surprised at the low figure you have offered. Can you tell me what went into the salary decision?"

You may discover that the employer's hands are tied by salary caps or by the current salaries of company employees with positions similar to the one you are applying for.

In this case, you might try negotiating along other angles:

- **A signing bonus:** This is a one-time, lump-sum figure that an employer may add to your salary at the time that you accept the position. While it may make you feel better going in, you receive it only once, and that uncomfortably low salary remains the same.
- **A rewritten job description with increased responsibilities:** If the employer is unwilling to pay the salary you want for the job he is offering, you might try changing the job description to include more responsibilities and thereby warrant a higher salary.
- **The performance-based bonus:** Many positions offer year-end or end-of-quarter bonuses which are often based upon job performance (number of products sold, marketing goals met, and so on). When discussing the size of the bonus, ask for a review of the bonus size over the past five years. This gives you a realistic estimate of this year's bonus potential.
- **A short-term review of performance:** Offer to prove how good you are. Ask for a review of your job performance after 60, 90, or 120 days. Get a guarantee for an increase in salary if the review is positive.
- **A more prestigious job title:** While this does nothing to help your wallet size, it may be meaningful to you to have a better job title. This can help in future job searches or future salary negotiations.

Focus on the Salary Focus your negotiations on the basic salary figure first. Remember that all future raises are based upon the salary figure that you agree to as you enter the job. The lower the figure you accept going in, the less money you could be paid throughout your career.

BENEFITS YOUR PACKAGE MAY INCLUDE

The benefits package included in your offer can play a significant part in your negotiation and decision-making process. While many companies offer a standard benefits package to all employees, it is always wise to consider your benefits options during negotiations. In general, the higher your position, the more possibilities you have for perks and additional benefits.

You Might Have to Ask In many cases, certain benefits are not offered to employees unless employees specifically request them. Request information on all benefits before accepting a job.

Consider this list of potential benefits and ask whether they might be a part of your package when you are in the negotiating phase of the job offer:

- **Medical Insurance**

  Key questions to consider: Does the company offer choices of coverage or "cafeteria-style" flexible plans? What proportion of the coverage is paid by the company? What medical conditions are covered, and what are the deductibles?

- **Dental Insurance**

  Key questions to consider: Can you choose your own provider? What are the deductibles? What procedures are covered?

- **Life Insurance**

  Key question to consider: Is supplemental coverage available?

- **Disability Insurance**

  Key questions to consider: How does the company define "disability"? Is short-term disability available?

- **Pension or 401(k) Plans**

  Key questions to consider: How long must you be employed before you can contribute? Does the employer match a certain percentage of the amount?

- **Vacation Time**
- **Personal Days**
- **Sick Leave**
- **Training Programs**

  Key question to consider: Does the company support attendance in seminars and training programs?

- **Tuition Reimbursement**

  Key questions to consider: Does the company pay for job-related courses? If so, what percentage of expense is covered?

- **Profit Sharing**
- **Stock Options**
- **Company Car**

  Key questions to consider: What are the restrictions for usage? Is the car available for personal use?

- **Car Allowance**

  Key question to consider: Does the company cover mileage, insurance, gas, and maintenance?

- **Club Memberships**
- **Expense Account**
- **Child Care**

  Key questions to consider: Does the company offer a day-care center on the premises? Are child care expenses reimbursed?

- **Parental Leave**

  Key question to consider: Does the company offer paid leave to one or both parents?

- **Counseling Services**

SUMMARY

In this lesson you learned of potential benefits options and received tips for negotiating aspects of the job offer other than salary.

EVALUATING THE JOB OFFER

In this lesson you learn effective techniques for evaluating job offers and for making decisions concerning difficult or multiple offers.

The time has come when all of your hard work and interviewing stress have paid off. The company is convinced that you are the best person for the job. It may happen on the first or second interview, but most likely not before the third. You finally hear those words you've waited so long to hear: "We feel you would make a solid contribution here. We'd like to make you an offer."

Hold Your Horses Before accepting or rejecting an offer, take a deep breath. No job should be accepted on the spot, no matter how good it may sound. Ask for a couple of days to consider it.

This is the appropriate time for the interviewer to begin salary discussions. (See Lesson 17, "Salary Negotiation," for tips on handling the salary issue.)

But the amount of take-home pay and benefits coverage you receive are really only a small part of any job offer. There are several other very important factors to evaluate when considering any job offer:

THE EIGHT MOST IMPORTANT ASPECTS TO CONSIDER IN A JOB OFFER

1. Will the job give me opportunities to grow?

   Contemplate the importance of career growth for your future happiness. Are you willing to wait a long time for a promotion? How frequently do performance and salary reviews occur, and on what factors are they based? Will you have to leave the company and go elsewhere in order to move into a higher position? What are the potential job titles you might move up into in the company that is making you the offer? How important is financial growth to you and your family?

2. Is the company on the rise and does it offer stability?

   What is the company's financial picture? Does it offer relative stability in today's unstable work world? Are there plans for new products, acquisitions, or a broadening scope? What are the plans for mergers, reorganizations, and downsizings? When was the last time the company reorganized, and did that reorganization affect the direction of your new position or department?

3. Will the position be interesting and challenging?

   Don't shoot for a position for which you are overqualified just because you know you will be able to handle it. Go for a position that offers career growth, if growth is important to you. Too many people underestimate themselves, fearing that employers only make job offers to people who have already mastered all aspects of a job.

4. Do I fit into the corporate culture?

   Evaluate the type of environment in which you thrive. Is it the climate of a company that is demanding, stressful, high-energy, and high-pressure? Or do you prefer a slower-paced, laid-back, gentler setting in which to work? Think of the situation that will keep you happy longest, because burn-out strikes quickly when one is either highly stressed or extremely bored.

5. Are the hours flexible, and do they match my needs?

   Some positions offer a great salary, but demand a 60- or 70-hour work week that leaves little time for friends and family. Other positions offer a flexible schedule or fewer hours, but less growth potential. Weigh the importance of these factors on your lifestyle and factor it into your decision.

6. Does the position involve travel?

   Depending upon your lifestyle and family obligations, you may be looking for a chance to do some traveling, or this may be something you want to avoid. Clarify your travel obligations as specifically as possible with the employer before making your decision.

7. Is the company in a convenient location?

   Will working for this company involve a long daily commute? Does it involve a relocation to another part of the country, and if so, how does the cost of living relate to the salary offer? How will this affect your family obligations and time commitments?

8. Will I enjoy working for my new boss?

What kind of management style does your new boss have? Does communication seem to flow freely? Are ideas and alternate viewpoints accepted easily? Will credit be given where credit is due? Is there a big difference in personality styles between you?

These are important factors to consider, yet it is also wise to remember that this person may not be your boss forever. There's always a chance for a change in management, for better or for worse.

DON'T SET YOUR SIGHTS TOO LOW

Don't accept the first job offer that comes along just because it is there. If you have received one job offer, you can receive more. Do not underestimate what you have to offer an employer. Evaluate your values, interests, skills, and accomplishments and find a position that will make you happy.

Don't Settle Accepting something that falls short of your goals will only lead to another, more difficult job search that will come up all too soon. It may lead to a feeling of failure and low self-esteem, which will only impede your next job search.

GENERATING MULTIPLE OFFERS

While the dream of many job seekers is to have the luxury of choosing from several good offers, many stop working hard at seeking a job once a potential offer looms on the horizon. They tend to relax and wallow in the comfort of the impending good fortune.

However, a potential offer should stimulate you to work even harder at making contacts and securing job interviews. With several irons in the fire, one solid job offer may be parlayed into an opportunity to choose among several.

When an offer comes in from company A, it is time to evaluate not only company A but the other companies you have interviewed with as well. If companies B and C were higher on your list of potential companies but neither has given you a firm offer, call them on the telephone right away.

Say something like,

> "I'm calling you because after meeting with you last week, I have received a job offer from another company. I'd prefer not to make a decision on that job offer without having the chance to talk with you again. I was very impressed with your company and intrigued by the challenges of the position we discussed. Might we meet again before the end of the week?"

This telephone call must be carefully worded to avoid several fatal mistakes:

- Do not put company B or C on the spot by asking, "Can you make me a better offer?" or "Was I a strong candidate for your position?"
- Do not strong-arm the other companies. Flatter them with your phone call rather than threatening them with your other offer.
- Do not in any way belittle the offer that you received from company A. That only reduces your negotiating power. In other words, don't say, "I received an offer from company A, but I'd much prefer working for you at company B."

- Be very specific about what you want. It is important to end your explanation with a suggestion for action. Rather than being vague by saying, "Do you think there is anything we could work out?" give your contacts at companies B and C a suggested next step, as in "Might we meet again in the next couple of days to discuss the possibilities?"

WEIGHING MULTIPLE OFFERS

Of course, the tactic of generating multiple offers may put you smack in the middle of a very happy dilemma, that of having two or three simultaneous job offers each of which offers several positives.

There is no better method of settling this quandary than the old tried-and-true method of putting the details down in black and white. Draw a line down the center of a paper and list the positives of an offer on one side and the negatives on the other. Weigh their importance to you by assigning each a number: 1 to 10 for the positives, and –1 to –10 for the negatives. While this may not create an instant and easy "eureka" type decision, it might clarify things enough to make your decision a little less overwhelming.

ACCEPTING A NEW POSITION

The key thing to remember in accepting any job is to have the terms of the offer given to you in writing. It is not an imposition to request the offer in writing, in fact, it is quite a standard practice. It is your absolute assurance that the terms you discussed in the offer negotiation still stand.

When you accept the position verbally, you might also request that the person making the offer clarify the terms in detail with you one more time. If any important information is left out, mention it by saying, "And we had also agreed upon a tuition reimbursement program for all education related to my position. Is that correct?" Do not assume that what you agreed upon earlier still stands unless you hear it again when you accept the position.

RESIGNING FROM YOUR CURRENT POSITION

Even the most difficult job situation should be left graciously and courteously. This is not the time to tell your boss what you really think of him or to offend your ex co-workers by assigning blame. Even weak bridges should not be burned!

A formal, brief resignation letter should be given to your current boss. Do not discuss any negative reasons for your leaving. Simply say that the new offer provides you with new challenges and opportunities. Your letter and discussion should be positive in all respects.

Such Sweet Sorrow If you are leaving on good terms, take the time to continue your contacts with your former co-workers and superiors. They might be useful networking contacts for you in future job searches.

SUMMARY

In this lesson you learned how to evaluate job offers and how to turn a single job offer into wider opportunities. You also learned to make a gracious and positive exit from your former company as you prepare to begin your new job.

Finding Information on Companies: Printed Sources of Corporate Profiles

Your local public library is an excellent source of information on both local and national companies. Some sources list extensive information about companies, including names and telephone numbers of key executives. Others give only a brief overview of the firm. Go to your library to begin your investigations. If you have trouble finding the right source, ask a reference librarian for help.

The Adams Job Almanac
Adams Media Corporation, Holbrook, MA
Includes information on over 10,000 companies.

The Almanac of American Employers
Corporate Jobs Outlook, Boerne, TX
Lists 500 large companies and provides profiles on salaries, benefits, and financial standing.

America's Fastest Growing Employers
Adams Media Corporation, Holbrook, MA
Offers profiles on nearly 300 companies.

Corporate Yellow Book
Monitor Leadership Directories, New York, NY
Provides information on over 1,000 companies and 7,000 subsidiary companies that are manufacturers, service businesses, or utilities.

Directory of Corporate Affiliations
National Register Publishing
New Providence, NJ
Several volumes of information regarding parent companies and their subsidiaries.

Directory of Leading Private Companies
National Register Publishing Company, Wilmette, IL
Provides profiles on over 7,000 private U.S. companies.

Hoover's Handbook of American Business 1997
The Reference Press, Austin, TX
Offers profiles of over 500 U.S. companies.

Hoover's Handbook of World Business 1995-96
The Reference Press, Austin, TX
Provides information on major European, Asian, Latin American, and Canadian companies that employ Americans in the U.S. and overseas.

International Directory of Company Histories
St. James Press, Chicago, IL
Offers detailed histories on thousands of companies around the world.

Million Dollar Directory
Dun & Bradstreet, Parsippany, NJ
Includes brief profiles on thousands of businesses in a broad range of industries. Also look for Dun's regional and other directories.

Moody's Manuals
Moody's Investor Service, New York, NY
Offers detailed information on various corporations. Look for other Moody's publications.

Predicasts F&S Index of Corporations and Industries
Predicasts, Inc. Cleveland, OH
A weekly list of published articles organized by company name and industry. Online counterpart is PTS F&S Indexes.

The JobBank Series
Adams Media Corporation, Holbrook, MA
Provides detailed profiles of larger (over 50 employees) local companies in each of 20 major metropolitan areas.

The National JobBank
Adams Media Corporation, Holbrook, MA
Includes profiles on over 16,000 companies nationwide.

Standard & Poor's Corporation Records
Standard & Poor's, New York, NY
Descriptions of publicly held corporations including corporate background information and stock data.

Thomas' Register
Thomas Publishing Co.
Twenty-seven volumes of information on manufacturers and their products and services.

Ward's Business Directory
Gale Research, Detroit, MI
Six volumes of information on private and public U.S. companies of all sizes.

TARGETED SOURCES

Sources for Technical Companies:

Corporate Technology Directory
CorpTech, Woburn, MA
Describes the products and services of over 35,000 technology-related businesses.

Sales Guide to High Tech Companies
CorpTech, Woburn, MA
Includes profiles of over 3,000 companies.

Sources for Health Care and Medical Companies:

U.S. Medical Directory
U.S. Directory Service, Miami, FL
Provides information on hospitals, medical laboratories, and other medical facilities.

Hospital Phone Book
U.S. Directory Service, Miami, FL
Offers information on nearly 8,000 U.S. hospitals (both government and private).

Sources for Federal Organizations:

Federal Jobs, The Ultimate Guide
Arco Books, 1997, New York, NY
Includes detailed profiles on virtually all federal agencies and job descriptions for the most common positions within each agency.

Federal Yellow Book
Monitor Leadership Directories, Washington, DC
Offers useful information on federal agencies and departments.

U.S. Government Manual
U.S. Government Printing Office, Washington, DC
Offers profiles of federal agencies and organization charts for the various departments.

Washington Information Directory
Congressional Quarterly Inc., Washington, DC
Offers information on federal agencies and nongovernmental organizations in the DC area.

Washington '97
Columbia Books, New York, NY
Offers information on key Washington-area organizations, both private- and public-sector.

Sources for Small or Private Companies:

Hoover's Handbook of Emerging Companies 1995
The Reference Press, Austin, TX
Offers profiles on 250 smaller companies with solid growth rates.

Hoover's Guide to Private Companies
The Reference Press, Austin, TX
Hundreds of profiles on private enterprises.

Sources of Industry Information:

Standard & Poor's Industry Surveys
Standard & Poor's, New York, NY
Provides history and basic information on various industries. Published weekly.

The 1997 Information Please Business Almanac and Desk Reference
Houghton Mifflin, New York, NY
Offers various information on industries and business.

APPENDIX

B

Finding Information on Companies: Online Sources of Corporate Profiles

While the local library offers a full supply of printed information on corporations and industries, you may find plenty of online sources useful as well. Although the list of sites is nearly endless and is growing steadily, this appendix lists some of the larger, tried-and-true sites offering information on corporations. One word of caution: The charges for some of these services can be rather steep. Check all costs carefully before you proceed with your research.

The Business Job Finder
(http://www.cob.ohio-state.edu/dept/fin/osujobs.htm)
You can find company profiles and links to other career sites through "Career Reference."

Commercenet
(http://www.commerce.net)
An index of the Web sites of many major businesses. Offers quarterly-earnings data, annual reports, promotional and product information, and links to other sites.

Dun & Bradstreet
(http://www.dbisna.com)
A database of corporate profiles and financial information on specific companies. One business background report costs about $20.

E-Span
(http://www.espan.com or http://www.careercompanion.com)
Can be accessed directly through the Net or through CompuServe and AOL. Its Career Companion includes profiles for at least 75 companies.

Hoover's Online
(http://www.hoovers.com)
A Web site for Hoover's Reference Press and Company Reports. Provides free access to search for information on over 9,000 companies. Also offers the weekly newsletter, *BIZBUZZ*, and a directory of over 1,300 corporations that can be found on the Web.

Louisiana State University Library: U.S. Federal Government Agency Directory
(http://www.lib.lsu.edu/gov/fedgov.html)
Provides links to federal government departments and agencies. Includes independent and quasi-official agencies.

Med Search America
(http://www.medsearch.com)
Offers profiles of health-care employers as well as many other features related to the health-care industry.

Yahoo! Business Directory
(http://www.yahoo.com/business)
An easy-to-use directory for business information and organizations on the Web.

LIST OF ADDITIONAL INTUITIVE AND LEARNED SKILLS

Find the most forceful terms with which to describe your own skills as you prepare your two-minute bio and gear up for your interviews.

INTUITIVE SKILLS TERMS

Adaptability
Adventurousness
Analysis
Artistic
Assembling
Assertiveness
Assessment
Coaching
Communicating
Composing
Conceptualizing
Coordinating
Courage
Creativity
Curiosity
Decision making
Designing
Detail-orientation
Dexterity
Diagnosing
Diplomacy
Directing Others
Discretion
Efficiency

Evaluating
Follow Through
Foresight
Imagination
Implementing
Independence
Individualism
Initiative
Innovation
Inventiveness
Leadership
Listening
Management
Motivating
Negotiating
Objectivity
Observing
Orderliness
Organization
Outgoingness
Patience
Perseverance
Persuasiveness
Planning
Prioritizing
Public Speaking
Receptivity
Resourcefulness
Risk Taking
Self-starting
Selling
Showmanship
Sincerity
Stamina
Supervising
Teaching
Team Building
Thoroughness
Time Management
Troubleshooting

Learned Skills Terms

Accounting
Actuarial
Administration
Benefits
Budgeting
Commercial Lending
Compensation
Computer Processing
Computer Programming
Consulting
Contracts
Counseling
Data Processing
Distribution
Drafting
Editing
Foreign Languages
Formulating Policies
Fund-raising
Health Care
Human Resources
Interviewing
Instructing
Labor Relations
Laboratory Work
Law
Letter Writing
Litigation
Lobbying
Machinery Operation
Manufacturing
Marketing
Materials Management
Medicine
Mortgage Brokering
Product Development
Promotion
Public Relations
Purchasing
Real Estate
Recruiting
Research
Scheduling
Training
Technical Writing
Writing Proposals

INDEX

A

accepting job offers, 138-139
accessories for men and women, 52-54
accomplishments, 6
  answering questions, 82
  skill identification, 7-13
affiliations, illegal questions, 107
age
  illegal questions, 104
  obstacles, overcoming, 70-71
answering questions, 78
  accomplishments, 6
  co-workers, former, 84
  examples, using, 85, 90-95
  guidelines, 79-89
  nervousness, 59
  panel interviews, 35-36
  practicing, 89
  salary, 122-123
  samples, 82-88, 92-94
  stress interviews, 34
  see also illegal employment questions
appearance, 48-46
arrival times, 24
  tardiness, 66
asking questions
  interview strategies, 64-65
  interviewees, 5, 81
    salary, 121-122
    preparation, 22-23
  interviewers, 78-79
  see also interviewees; questions to ask
assumed names, illegal questions, 105

B - C

background, 14-15
  biographies, 15-18
  noises in telephone interviews, 32
  questions, 81-82
benefits (employment), 130-131
biographies, 15-18
body language, 59-61
bonuses, 129
briefcases, 52-54, 58, 67
business cards, asking for, 65
careers, changing, 72, 134
chewing gum, 56
citizenship, illegal questions, 105-106
closings
  interviews, 61
  thank-you notes, 115-116
clothing, 24, 48-52
communication skills, 48
  desirable qualities, 42
  dominating conversations, 66
  overformal language, 67
  phrasing questions, 96-98
  rambling, 66
  slang language, 67
  thank-you notes, 109-110
companies
  culture as job offer consideration, 135
  industry information, 144-146
  researching, 20, 64
confidence, *see* self-confidence
criminal history, illegal questions, 106
current jobs, resigning, 139

D - F

dental insurance, 131
disabilities
  disability insurance, 131
  illegal questions, 105
distractions
  background noises during telephone interviews, 32
  during interviews, 46, 67
downsizing, 86
dress, 24, 48-54, 63

education
  legality of questions, 106
  obstacles, overcoming, 75-76
employment history, gaps, 73-74
ending interviews, 61
enthusiasm at interviews, 28, 30, 65
evaluating interviewees, 40-44, 94-95
experience
  evaluating interviewees, 40
  legality of questions, 106
eye contact
  nonverbal communication, 60
  panel interviews, 36

federal agencies, profiles, 143-144
feedback, asking for, 68
flexibility
  interview strategies, 65-66
  job offer considerations, 135
follow-up action
  interview strategies, 64-65
  thank-you notes, 109-118
formatting thank-you notes, 111

G - I

gaps in employment, overcoming, 73-74
gestures (hands), 59-60

hairstyles, 49, 56
hand gestures, 59-60
handshakes
  ending interviews, 61
  meeting interviewers, 57
  panel interviews, 35
health care company profiles, 143
hiring
  interviews, 28-29
  obstacles, 70-76
hygiene, preparing for interviews, 55-56

illegal employment questions, 103-108
image, 48
  etiquette, 55
  hygiene, 55-56
insurance
  dental, 131
  disability, 131
  life, 131
  medical, 130
integrity, 42-43
interests
  job offer considerations, 134
  question samples, 85-86
Internet, researching companies, 20
interpersonal skills, 44
interruptions during interviews, 46, 67
interviewees
  questions to ask, 96-102
  strengths, 21-22
interviewers
  confirmation interviews, 30
  first names, using, 65
  hiring interviews, 29
  panel discussions, 35
  questions
    accomplishments, 6, 9-10
    background, 14-15
  screening interviews, 28
  stress interviews, 34
  see also evaluating interviewees
interviews
  arrival times, 24
  behaviors and topics to avoid, 66-68
  beginning, 56-58
  company-related influences, 45-47
  confirmation interviews, length of interview, 30
  ending, 61
  essential items, 25
  nonverbal communication, 26
  reception areas, 56-57
  types, 28-38
intuitive skills, 9-10, 147-148

J - L

job changes, frequency, overcoming, 74
job descriptions, negotiating, 129
job offers
  accepting, 138-139
  considerations, 134-136
  multiple offers
    considerations, 138
    obtaining, 136-138
  resigning from jobs, 139
job seekers, *see* interviewees
job titles, negotiating, 129

leadership skills, 95
learned skills, 8-9, 149
legal aspects of interview questions, 104-108
length of interview, 30
library research on companies, 20
life insurance, 131
listening
  interview strategies, 63
  phone interviews, 33
  verbal affirmations, 60
location as job offer considerations, 135

M - P

makeup (women), 49
management styles as job offer considerations, 136
marital status, illegal questions, 104
market value and salary negotiations, 124-125
mealtime interviews, 37-38
medical insurance, 130
men, appearance, 49-52, 56
military service, illegal questions, 107
minimum requirements for salary, 120-121
motivation
  desirable qualities, 41-42
  illustrating through example, 95
multiple job offers, 136-138

negative statements
  former employers/co-workers, 84
  hiring interviews, 29
  screening interviews, 27
negotiating
  bonuses, 129
  job descriptions, 129
  salaries, 120-126
noises during telephone interviews, 32
nonverbal communication, 26, 35-36, 59-61
note-taking during interview, 64-65, 97
notes (thank-you), 29, 109-118

obstacles (work history), overcoming, 71-77
offers
accepting, 138
considerations, 134-136
multiple, 136-138
others, mentioning, 67
quitting current jobs, 139
online resources
company profiles, 145-146
researching companies, 20
overformal language, 67
overqualifications, 72

panel interviews, 35-36
pension plans, 131
performance-based bonuses, negotiating, 129
personal qualities to emphasize, 41-44
personality traits, 94-95
phrasing questions, 97-98
preparing for interviews, 3-5, 19-25
problem-solving skills, 84, 99
professionalism, 65-66

Q - R

questions
answer guidelines, 85
illegal, 103-108
interviewees, 64, 96-98,100-102
preparation, 5, 22-23
interviewers, 78
accomplishments, 6
background, 14-15
guidelines, 79-89
panel discussions, 35-36
salary, 123
skills, 9-10
stress interviews, 34
samples, 81-89, 92-93
quitting current job, 139

race, illegal questions, 103
rapport, building, 30, 36
receptionists, speaking to, 56-57
reducing stress, 4-5
references, legality of questions, 107-108
relatives, illegal questions, 106
religion, illegal questions, 104
researching companies, 20
industry information, 144
interview strategies, 64-65
job openings, 21
preparing for interviews, 5
profiles, 140-144
resigning from jobs, 139
resources
company profiles, 140-144
federal agencies, 143-144
questions to ask, 101
role-playing, 23

S

salary
appropriate questions, 100
discussing, 67, 121-125
history, 73
negotiating, 119-126
salutations, 65
screening interviews, 27-28
self-confidence, 45
lack of, 67
sexual orientation, illegal questions, 104
signing bonuses, 129
sites (Web), company profiles, 145-146
skills, 7-13
illustrating through examples, 90-95
interviewers' evaluations, 40
intuitive skills, 9-10, 147-148
learned skills, 8-9, 149
overcoming obstacles, 76-77
screening interviews, 27
transferable, 71
underqualifications, 71
slang language, 67
smoking, 37, 56
strategies for interviews, 62-68
strengths
illustrating through examples, 90-93
knowing, 21-22
question samples, 85, 92-93
stress during interviews, 4-5
suits, 50-52
supervisors
former, answering questions, 84, 87
meeting, 100

T - Z

taking notes, 97
technical company profiles, 143
telephone interviews, 31-33
terminations, employment, 75, 86
thank-you notes, 109-118
confirmation interviews, 30
hiring interviews, 29
mealtime interviews, 38
timing
arrivals, 24, 66
salary discussions, 121-122
thank-you notes, 109-110
titles, jobs, negotiating, 129
transferable skills, 71
travel as job offer consideration, 135

verbal affirmations, listening, 60
voice tone in telephone interviews, 33
volunteer work, 71

Web sites, company profiles, 145-146
women
accessories and clothing, 52-54
hairstyles, 49, 56
makeup, 49